At Issue

What Is the Future of the Music Industry?

Other Books in the At Issue Series:

Can Celebrities Change the World?

Disaster Planning

Disposal of the Dead

Does the World Hate the U.S.?

Genetically Modified Food

Greenhouse Gases

Has Technology Increased Learning?

How Safe Is America's Infrastructure?

The Olympics

Polygamy

Should the U.S. Do Business with China?

Teen Smoking

The U.S. Policy on Cuba

What Is the Impact of E-Waste?

What Is the Impact of Tourism?

At Issue

What Is the Future of the Music Industry?

Roman Espejo, Book Editor

GREENHAVEN PRESS
A part of Gale, Cengage Learning

GALE
CENGAGE Learning™

Detroit • New York • San Francisco • New Haven, Conn • Waterville, Maine • London

Christine Nasso, *Publisher*
Elizabeth Des Chenes, *Managing Editor*

© 2009 Greenhaven Press, a part of Gale, Cengage Learning.

Gale and Greenhaven Press are registered trademarks used herein under license.

For more information, contact:
Greenhaven Press
27500 Drake Rd.
Farmington Hills, MI 48331-3535
Or you can visit our Internet site at gale.cengage.com

For product information and technology assistance, contact us at

Gale Customer Support, 1-800-877-4253
For permission to use material from this text or product, submit all requests online at www.cengage.com/permissions

Further permissions questions can be emailed to permissionrequest@cengage.com

Articles in Greenhaven Press anthologies are often edited for length to meet page requirements. In addition, original titles of these works are changed to clearly present the main thesis and to explicitly indicate the author's opinion. Every effort is made to ensure that Greenhaven Press accurately reflects the original intent of the authors. Every effort has been made to trace the owners of copyrighted material.

Cover photograph reproduced by permission of Brand X Pictures.

LIBRARY OF CONGRESS CATALOGING-IN-PUBLICATION DATA

What is the future of the music industry? / Roman Espejo, book editor.
    p. cm. -- (At issue)
Includes bibliographical references and index.
ISBN 978-0-7377-4110-0 (hardcover)
ISBN 978-0-7377-4111-7 (pbk.)
1. Sound recording industry. I. Espejo, Roman, 1977-
ML3790.W48 2008
381'.45780973--dc22

2008021555

Printed in the United States of America
2 3 4 5 6   14 13 12 11 10

ED179

Contents

Introduction   7

1. Declining Music Sales Threaten the Future   10
of the Music Industry
Ethan Smith

2. Poor Content and Marketing Threaten   16
the Future of the Music Industry
Chris Moreau

3. Digital Music Is the Future of the   20
Music Industry
Alice LaPlante

4. Retail Music Stores Must Adapt to the   31
Changing Music Industry
Hil Anderson

5. The Sound Quality of Music Is at Risk   35
in the Music Industry
Suhas Sreedhar

6. The CD Is Obsolete   46
Daniel B. Wood

7. The CD Is Not Obsolete   51
Daniel Gross

8. Vinyl Records Threaten the Future of CDs   55
Eliot Van Buskirk

9. Illegal File Sharing Threatens the Future   59
of the Music Industry
Recording Industry Association of America

10. Illegal File Sharing Enhances the Future   69
    of the Music Industry
    Sean Silverthorne

Organizations to Contact   75
Bibliography   79
Index   82

Introduction

Since 2000, sales of compact discs (CDs) have plummeted 40 percent in the United States, and illegal music downloads are at an all-time high. According to global market intelligence firm IDC, file sharing on peer-to-peer (P2P) services could be as high as a billion a day, dwarfing relatively conservative estimates of one to three billion a month. On the contrary, global digital music sales have increased 40 percent from 2006, with iPod manufacturer Apple positioning itself as the leading music retailer in April 2008. Its online music store, iTunes, rang in one-fifth of all music sales, trumping the CD sales of Wal-Mart for the first time.

Whether or not illegal music downloading is crippling the music industry is hotly debated, but it is evident that digital distribution of music is making waves. A growing number of bands and artists are beginning to favor the format. Bands such as the White Stripes and Matchbox Twenty have released albums on universal serial bus (USB) drives, a format that is more digitally friendly than CDs. Furthermore, in October 2007, their recording contract with music company EMI fulfilled, pioneering British rock band Radiohead digitally released their latest studio album, *In Rainbows*, allowing consumers to choose the price they wish to pay, even if it was nothing. This outraged some industry experts, who believed that this was an egregious business misstep. However, a month later, Radiohead moved 1.2 million units at an average price of $8 per unit—a sum of which no music company would get a cut.

Nonetheless, adapting to the digitizing of music distribution has left music companies scrambling for solutions. Some insist that P2P file sharing is responsible for tumbling CD sales and have aggressively sued individuals who illegally share music files. In March 2007, the Recording Industry Association of America (RIAA) sent pre-litigation letters to 405 college students who were illegally sharing music at twenty-three universities, allowing them to settle monetarily and forgo going to court. Seven months later, in a key victory for the music industry, Jamie Thomas of Duluth, Minnesota, was successfully sued by six music companies for sharing twenty-four copyrighted songs on P2P service Kazaa, at the tune of $9,250 per track.

Other strategies the music industry is seeking to stem the revenue losses they attribute to P2P file sharing target the role of Internet service providers (ISPs). The Motion Picture Association of America (MPAA) proposes that ISPs filter their networks of pirated content to counter illegal movie downloads and other forms of Internet piracy, which the music industry attempted to do with P2P services in 2001. Also, Jim Griffin, digital music consultant and former head of the technology department of Geffen Records, is leading the creation of an ISP "piracy tax." In March 2008, Griffin was tapped by Warner Music Group to form, within three years, an organization dedicated to bundling a fee that acts as a tax for P2P file sharing—whether or not the Internet user illegally shares music—into monthly Internet service charges.

On the other end of the spectrum, numerous music retailers, record companies, and artists and bands are devising plans to make digital music even more accessible. Though its iTunes Store is a runaway success—and the most successful online music store by far—the *Financial Times* reported in March 2008 that Apple is currently in discussions with record labels to create an unlimited music plan that accompanies the purchase of an MP3 player. Microsoft, for instance, offers such a service at $15 per month for its iPod rival, Zune. And the aptly named online record label RCRD LBL, which was launched in late 2007, offers free music downloads in a blog format, in which its artists and bands are paid a fee between $500 and $5,000. For RCRD LBL, free music is the business model, and money is made from other streams of revenue, such as advertising. Moreover, more artists and bands are following Radiohead's lead by releasing digital-only tracks and offering MP3 downloads on their Web sites and on social networks such as MySpace.

These forays into digital music are innovative, but it is too soon to tell whether these new business models successfully harness the surge in digital music. In *At Issue: What Is the Future of the Music Industry?*, industry insiders, Internet experts, and music lovers discuss the future of music—how it will be distributed, how it will be played, even how it will sound—in a digital age.

1

Declining Music Sales Threaten the Future of the Music Industry

Ethan Smith

Ethan Smith is a staff reporter for the Wall Street Journal.

Since 2000, music sales have been in a sharp decline, leading to the dissolution of specialty music retailers, including the music retailer giant Tower Records. Although the sales of digital downloads—especially of individual songs on iTunes—have risen more than 50 percent between 2006 and 2007, it has not been enough to compensate for the dramatically dropping sale of compact discs. Retailers and industry insiders allege that record companies are not producing blockbuster albums, and sales of what are considered hit albums today do not come close to reaching numbers they have in the past. Some believe that illegal downloads, which have reached a billion songs a month, are clearly linked to these dwindling figures.

In a dramatic acceleration of the seven-year sales decline [since 2000] that has battered the music industry, compactdisc sales for the first three months of this year [2007] plunged 20% from a year earlier, the latest sign of the seismic shift in the way consumers acquire music.

The sharp slide in sales of CDs, which still account for more than 85% of music sold, has far eclipsed the growth in sales of digital downloads, which were supposed to have been the industry's salvation.

Ethan Smith, "Sales of Music, Long in Decline, Plunge Sharply" *Wall Street Journal*, March 21, 2007. Republished with permission of *The Wall Street Journal*, conveyed through Copyright Clearance Center, Inc.

The slide stems from the confluence of long-simmering factors that are now feeding off each other, including the demise of specialty music retailers like longtime music mecca Tower Records. About 800 music stores, including Tower's 89 locations, closed in 2006 alone.

Apple Inc.'s sale of around 100 million iPods shows that music remains a powerful force in the lives of consumers. But because of the Internet, those consumers have more ways to obtain music now than they did a decade ago, when walking into a store and buying it was the only option.

Today, popular songs and albums—and countless lesser-known works—can be easily found online, in either legal or pirated forms. While the music industry hopes that those songs will be purchased through legal services like Apple's iTunes Store, consumers can often listen to them on MySpace pages or download them free from other sources, such as so-called MP3 blogs.

Little More Than Advertisements

Jeff Rabhan, who manages artists and music producers including Jermaine Dupri, Kelis and Elliott Yamin, says CDs have become little more than advertisements for more-lucrative goods like concert tickets and T-shirts. "Sales are so down and so off that, as a manager, I look at a CD as part of the marketing of an artist, more than as an income stream," says Mr. Rabhan. "It's the vehicle that drives the tour, the merchandise, building the brand, and that's it. There's no money."

The music industry has found itself almost powerless in the face of this shift. Its struggles are hardly unique in the media world. The film, TV and publishing industries are also finding it hard to adapt to the digital age. Though consumers are exposed to more media in more ways than ever before, the challenge for media companies is finding a way to make money from all that exposure. Newspaper publishers, for example, are finding that their Internet advertising isn't growing fast enough to replace the loss of traditional print ads.

In recent weeks, the music industry has posted some of the weakest sales it has ever recorded. This year has already seen the two lowest-selling No. 1 albums since Nielsen Sound-Scan, which tracks music sales, was launched in 1991.

In general, even today's big titles are stalling out far earlier than they did a few years ago.

One week, *American Idol* runner-up Chris Daughtry's rock band sold just 65,000 copies of its chart-topping album; another week, the "Dreamgirls" movie soundtrack sold a mere 60,000. As recently as 2005, there were many weeks when such tallies wouldn't have been enough to crack the top 30 sellers. In prior years, it wasn't uncommon for a No. 1 record to sell 500,000 or 600,000 copies a week.

In general, even today's big titles are stalling out far earlier than they did a few years ago.

The music industry has been banking on the rise of digital music to compensate for inevitable drops in sales of CDs. Apple's 2003 launch of its iTunes Store was greeted as a new day in music retailing, one that would allow fans to conveniently and quickly snap up large amounts of music from limitless virtual shelves.

It hasn't worked out that way—at least so far. Digital sales of individual songs this year [in 2007] have risen 54% from a year earlier to 173.4 million, according to Nielsen SoundScan. But that's nowhere near enough to offset the 20% decline from a year ago in CD sales to 81.5 million units. Overall, sales of all music—digital and physical—are down 10% this year. And even including sales of ringtones, subscription services and other "ancillary" goods, sales are still down 9%, according to one estimate; some recording executives have privately questioned that figure, which was included in a recent report by Pali Research.

Meanwhile, one billion songs a month are traded on illegal file-sharing networks, according to BigChampagne LLC.

Adding to the music industry's misery, CD prices have fallen amid pressure for cheaper prices from big-box retailers like Wal-Mart and others. That pressure is feeding through to record labels' bottom lines. As the market has deteriorated, Warner Music Group Corp., which reported a 74% drop in profits for the fourth quarter of 2006, is expected to report little relief in the first quarter of this year [2007].

Looking at unit sales alone "flatters the situation," says Simon Wright, chief executive of Virgin Entertainment Group International, which runs 14 Virgin Megastore locations in North America and 250 worldwide. "In value terms, the market's down 25%, probably." Virgin's music sales have increased slightly this year, he says, thanks to the demise of chief competitor Tower, and to a mix of fashion and "lifestyle" products designed to attract customers.

The Shakeout Among Music Retailers

Perhaps the biggest factor in the latest chapter of the music industry's struggle is the shakeout among music retailers. As recently as a decade ago, specialty stores like Tower Records were must-shop destinations for fans looking for both big hits and older catalog titles. But retailers like Wal-Mart Stores Inc. and Best Buy Co. took away the hits business by undercutting the chains on price. Today such megaretailers represent about 65% of the retail market, up from 20% a decade ago, music-distribution executives estimate. And digital-music piracy, which has been rife since the rise of the original Napster file-sharing service, has allowed many would-be music buyers to fill their CD racks or digital-music players without ever venturing into a store.

Late last year [in 2007], Tower Records closed its doors, after filing for bankruptcy-court protection in August. Earlier in 2006, following a bankruptcy filing, Musicland Holding Corp., which owned the Sam Goody chain, closed 500 of its 900 locations. And recently, Trans World Entertainment Corp., which operates the FYE and Coconuts chains, among others, began closing 134 of its 1,087 locations.

But even at the outlets that are still open, business has suffered. Executives at Trans World, based in Albany, N.Y., told analysts ... that sales of music at its stores declined 14% in the last quarter of 2006. For the year, music represented just 44% of the company's sales, down from 54% in 2005. For the final quarter of the year, music represented just 38% of its sales.

Retailers and others say record labels failed to deliver big sellers.

Joe Nardone Jr., who owns the independent 10-store Gallery of Sound chain in Pennsylvania, says he is trying to make up for declining sales of new music by emphasizing used CDs, which he calls "a more consistent business." For now, though, he says used discs represent less than 10% of his business—not nearly enough to offset the declines.

Retailers and others say record labels have failed to deliver big sellers. And even the hits aren't what they used to be. Norah Jones's "Not Too Late" has sold just shy of 1.1 million copies since it was released six weeks ago. Her previous album, "Feels Like Home," sold more than 2.2 million copies in the same period after its 2004 release.

"Even when you have a good release like Norah Jones, maybe the environment is so bad you can't turn it around," says Richard Greenfield, an analyst at Pali Research.

Meanwhile, with music sales sliding for the first time even at some big-box chains, Best Buy has been quietly reducing the floor space it dedicates to music, according to music-distribution executives.

Whether Wal-Mart and others will follow suit isn't clear, but if they do, it could spell more trouble for the record companies. The big-box chains already stocked far fewer titles than did the fading specialty retailers. As a result, it is harder for consumers to find and purchase older titles in stores.

2

Poor Content and Marketing Threaten the Future of the Music Industry

Chris Moreau

Chris Moreau is a writer and musician based in Springfield, Virginia.

Although repetitive purchasing—from vinyl records to cassette tapes to compact discs—may have artificially boosted album sales in previous decades, the current downward slide of music sales is caused by the music industry's inability to focus on content, which fails on two accounts. First, the industry places too much emphasis on the content of too few artists, many of which are no longer relevant. Second, the industry seems to have forgotten how to produce and market quality content. In order to reverse the music sales slump, record companies must stop promoting "big acts" only and focus more on music itself.

Since the advent of the MP3 format for music, the music industry has been whining about the money it has "lost" due to piracy. Let's take a look at that.

First, the facts. Sales of CDs in 2007 were down 15% compared to 2006, based on number of units moved. The trend has continued down for years and is expected to continue in that direction. Sales of digital tracks are up 45% over that same one year. 45% is a lot, I think you'll agree. If you assume

Chris Moreau, "Online Music Sales," ChrisMoreau.com, January 8, 2008. Reproduced by permission.

that 10 digital tracks are the equivalent of a single CD, then the decline in CD sales lands at around 9.5%. Not as bad, but still a significant decline.

Now, some thoughts. In the early '70s my older brother bought me my first LP, it was *Sittin' In* by Loggins & Messina. Being just a lad, I treated my vinyl badly and had to replace it with allowance money later in the decade. Then I got a cassette tape so I could listen to it in the tape deck in my beat-up MG. Later, when I was in college, the format changed again so I bought it on CD. That's four different purchases of the same bit of music. The original purchase was in good faith. The initial replacement was valid, given the technology of the day and the dirty fingers of the owner. But the latter two purchases were due to format changes, first to tape and then to digital. The artist and the music industry asked me to dip into my pocket two additional times just to keep up.

How many times did the entire baby boomer generation purchase copies of *Dark Side of the Moon*? If I take a stab, I count four: once for the original purchase on vinyl, once on eight-track so they could listen to it in the GTO, once on cassette so they could listen to it in the station wagon, once on CD. Over the years, the music industry has morphed into a machine that relies heavily on the sales of its catalog rather than focusing on creating new and (this is important) worthwhile music. With each successive change in format, sales of the back catalog jumped as customers reloaded their own collections with the latest format.

Could it be that the entire industry's gross sales have been artificially inflated over the decades by repetitive buying? Maybe the base level of consumption is lower than anyone thought and it's only now becoming apparent as repetitive purchasing falls off.

Too Much Focus on the Known

In addition to a reliance on re-purchases, in my view Big Music has neglected to focus on sowing seeds for its future. Far too much emphasis has been placed on getting another U2 CD, another Rolling Stones CD, another Madonna CD out. While each of these bands or artists is a guaranteed seller, none of them has been relevant for years, maybe a decade.

Album sales have plunged due to lousy content and ineffective marketing by an industry incapable of looking beyond this year's bottom line.

So who are the new players? There are a few: John Mayer, Radiohead, Diddy, Alicia Keys, even Justin Timberlake or Green Day. Even this is a list of artists who have been in the saddle for years. It's not enough. There is too much focus on the known and not enough on the potential. For each of these artists, I have purchased a CD once and probably ripped it so I could put it on my iPod. The important distinction here is that with this latest format change, from CD to MP3, I was able to change the format myself without having to repurchase the music again.

Given the rate of technology change, the ability of the masses to manage their digital collections themselves, and a huge industry's inability to manage (or even understand the ramifications of) said change quickly, it seems to me that the music industry should now focus on content. Find the talent and produce something I want to hear. Embrace content. An artist could conceivably produce a single on Friday and have it on a million iPods by Saturday night via the various digital music purveyors. This feels to me a lot like the '60s, when the 45 [type of vinyl record] reigned supreme. A young purchaser could run out and get the latest song he or she just heard on the radio for a buck. Likewise, if I hear something on the radio I can log onto iTunes when I get home and have it in an instant.

Bring me cool melody, a killer riff, a catchy hook, and I'll buy it. I know what I like and have the 99 cents to get what I want. Just bring it to me and find a way to let me know it's out there. I recently discovered a CD called *Jazzmatazz* by an artist named Guru, a fusion of Jazz and Hip Hop that's way cool. I looked it up on Amazon and found that there is a whole series of *Jazzmatazz* CDs. The first one came out in 1993, well over a decade ago. How did I miss this? How much more is out there that I've missed? All I hear about are the big acts, and frankly I've had enough of them.

Money has been lost due to piracy, for certain. But if a billion songs are traded online every month, that does not translate to a billion lost dollars to the music industry. If all online piracy were stopped today, some small percentage of that billion would be made up through legitimate channels.

Album sales have plunged due to lousy content and ineffective marketing by an industry incapable of looking beyond this year's bottom line, fiscal myopia. Take the long view, provide the content, embrace the future or the future will leave you behind. The fact that Tower Records has gone out of business should be an indicator, don't you think?

3

Digital Music Is the Future of the Music Industry

Alice LaPlante

Alice LaPlante is a technology journalist and author of Playing for Profit: How Digital Entertainment Is Making Big Business Out of Child's Play.

The music industry is going digital, and despite flagging compact disc sales, music consumption is growing. In order to turn profits in this digital world, different models of distribution for digital music are being explored, posing new challenges and creating new possibilities for record labels, music companies, digital media services, and artists themselves. For instance, digital downloads, available from Apple and Amazon, have exploded, and now there are subscription-based music services, such as Rhapsody. The rock band Radiohead also made digital music history—and profits—by offering its latest album online with an optional price tag. Digital downloads are a way of promoting both albums and the discovery of new music and artists, thus replacing mainstream radio, Rolling Stone, *and MTV as the authorities of what music should be listened to.*

Michael Bracy has a file on his Windows desktop labeled "solutions." In it, he's collected the many dozens of suggestions that have come to him over the years as policy director of the Future of Music Coalition on how to fix the music business. He occasionally reads through them with wry amusement.

Alice LaPlante, "MP3 Unplugged: Rethinking the Digital Music Future," *Information-Week*, January 31, 2008. www.informationweek.com. Reproduced by permission of CMP Media LLC.

"It's very sweet of people," said Bracy, who founded the nonprofit think tank that advocates for musical artists trying to make it in an increasingly technological world, "but the current business model has been completely shattered, and there is no single one-size-fits-all solution." However, he believes that despite all the industry negativity about this fact, "we're seeing unprecedented creativity and innovation that in the end will benefit both artists and consumers alike."

As evidence, Bracy points to all the technology-spurred experimentation with new business models. From the advertising-supported free music downloads offered by Spiral Frog, to subscription-based services such as Rhapsody, to Amazon engaging Apple in a head-to-head competition in the music download space, some of the best and brightest minds in both the technological and music fields are testing the waters to see how to make money from music, now that physical recorded media is going the way of the buffalo. "All the chaos actually spells incredibly good news," said Bracy.

Indeed, in the December [2007] issue of *Wired*, the musician David Byrne wrote a feature naming six different models that artists were pursuing to profitably get their music to consumers. These ranged from the traditional relationship with labels all the way to a do-it-yourself model in which the artist handles everything from recording to marketing to distribution.

One of the biggest music business news stories of 2007 was Radiohead releasing its latest album in digital form and giving music consumers the option of paying what they liked for it. . . . *Fortune* magazine called the move one of the "dumbest business moments" of the year, citing comScore numbers indicating that only 40% of consumers paid for it—and only paid a meager $6 each. Yet band member Thom Yorke pointed out that it netted the band $3 million. And others say that trying out new business models, and learning from failures as well as successes, is exactly what the industry should be doing.

"The industry shouldn't be searching for *the* answer, but should be pursuing all the very many possible ways there are for monetizing music," said Peter Faber, professor of marketing at the Wharton School of Business at the University of Pennsylvania.

"We have to rethink how we sell music, throw the rule book out the window, and open ourselves up to entirely new possibilities," agreed Paul Verna, senior analyst for media and entertainment for eMarketer.

Independent musicians, labels, and, increasingly, Web sites, are doing this. Some are trying the subscription model; others are attempting to market value-added services and products that are tied to sales of conventional albums; still others are blending digital downloads and physical media. "Unfortunately, there's a very strong herd mentality among the major labels, and the lack of variety in their practices is quite shocking given all the opportunities that are out there," said Faber.

"Everyone is both hopeful and uncertain about what we need to do to transform the music industry," said Samantha Murphy, a singer/songwriter and founder of samanthamurphy.com. Like a growing number of musicians, Murphy believes that the only way to evolve as an artist as well as a businessperson is to pursue a more populist business model based on using technology to cultivate more intimate relationships with consumers. "I'm convinced that people, when given the opportunity, will be willing to pay for the music they love," she said. "With so many smart and creative people working on this challenge, I'm sure we will succeed."

From Service to Product and Back Again

Until 130 years ago, music was a service—an entertainment experience provided by musicians to the public in a live venue. But with the invention of the phonograph, it was transformed, practically overnight, into a physical product: the record.

Colin Brumelle, a San Francisco-based musician and developer of software for musicians and record labels, pointed out that when the phonograph was invented in 1877, it was a radical invention able to, in Thomas Edison's own words, "annihilate time and space."

The response from the music business was immediate and alarmist. [Late American composer] John Philip Sousa wrote an essay titled "The Menace of Mechanical Music" that warned how recorded music would cause the entire music industry to go into a disastrous decline. "Of course, much of the subtext of this was economic," said Brumelle. "Musicians were understandably worried that recorded music would undercut their ability to command fees for performance."

Later, in the 1930s, radio caused the same upheaval, as the recorded music industry worried its business would be destroyed. Much later, the tape cassette, the first easily recordable media, caused widespread consternation. Indeed, the slogan of the British Phonographic Industry from a 1980s-era anti-piracy campaign was "Home Taping Is Killing Music." MP3 provoked the same outcry, as evidenced by the reaction to, and effective killing of Napster by the industry, in the early 2000s.

Although major labels are still selling hundreds of millions of CDs, those numbers have been declining rapidly and precipitously—largely due to the escalating popularity of digital downloads.

Once music was turned into a product, the business model for producing it was straightforward: record companies would invest in artists by paying them money upfront for the right to record and sell their music, and by spending the necessary funds on recording, marketing, and distribution of the physical disks that held that music. This investment was then recouped—and, under optimal circumstances, exceeded—by sales of the records. "In effect, the record labels acted simultaneously as investment banks and as marketing and distribution companies," said David Kusek, coauthor of *The Future of Music* and a VP at the Berklee College of Music.

But that model, everyone agrees, is now broken, largely due to the advent of the Internet, digital downloads, and other technological advances which have turned the physical product back into a service. Although major labels are still selling hundreds of millions of CDs, those numbers have been declining rapidly and precipitously—largely due to the escalating popularity of digital downloads.

Between 2006 and 2007 revenues from CD sales plummeted from $14 billion to $9 billion, according to James McQuivey, VP and principal analyst of consumer media technology for Forrester. And according to Nielsen SoundScan, in 2007 CD sales were down 5% over 2006, whereas digital track sales increased by a full 65% and digital album sales more than doubled to 33 million.

Moreover, the profit margins of the recorded music industry, which in the 1980s were 15% to 20%, have declined to less than 5% today, according to Plunkett Research's "Entertainment and Media Industry Trends and Statistics 2007."

"For years, people were willing to compensate the music labels for going to the hassle of finding the artists, organizing their best stuff in shiny plastic disks called albums, and promoting them," said McQuivey. But now that the Internet is providing consumers with another way to discover music, and there's no longer a need for the actual physical product, "consumers are suddenly much less willing to do this. They have the Internet and friends sending links, and all sorts of ways to listen to new songs. Suddenly, there's no role left for the labels."

Music Consumption, However, Is Growing

Yet despite all the woeful sounds tolling the death of the music business, in fact it is growing overall at a healthy rate. It is arguably only *recorded* music that is in trouble. eMarketer estimates that the worldwide market for recorded music, live music, and music publishing will exceed $67 billion by 2011, compared to $62 billion in 2007. But this 2.2% growth will come largely from online and mobile music, live concerts—where revenues are growing rapidly—and licensing of music for public performances, commercials, TV shows, films, and video games.

Indeed, overall music consumption seems to be dramatically on its way up. Bridge Ratings, which tracks the percentage of the U.S. population that consumes music, has seen dramatic increases. In 1980, only 20% of the population was actively consuming music; in 1990, it was 21%; in 2000 it was 26%; and in 2006 it was 32%. "On the face of it, that's impressive," said Verna. "But if you plot those figures against per capita music expenditure, you see a drastic decline." In other words, said Verna, more people listen to music, but they spend a lot less money while doing so.

"We live in an age where music is all around us. Music has proliferated across all these channels—commercials, video games, television shows, movies, amusement park rides—its part of what's in the air and it accompanies us no matter where we are or what we are doing," said Verna. "We expect to have our collections with us at all times, and in many ways, music is now taken for granted." Part of the problem is that people—especially younger people—simply don't believe they owe anyone anything for the privilege of listening to music, especially when that music exists in digital form. "It's not that they don't value it, just that they don't feel they need to pay for it," said Verna. "They simply don't think of this in moral terms. They've always gotten their music for free, and they don't see why that should change."

Thus although online music might seem to offer a "lifeline" to the major music labels, it's hard to say whether the escalating growth in digital downloads will fill the hole left by the disappearance of so much physical sales revenues, according to Dan Cryan, a music analyst with Screen Digest, a London-based media analyst firm.

"Yes, the Internet is facilitating discovery of new music and new artists by consumers," said Cryan, "but discovery on its own is pointless. Discovery that drives sales is what matters to the labels. And the underlying deal infrastructure that facilitates the sharing of revenues between the online services and traditional broadcast and recorded media players is not yet in place."

Telecom: The New Music Scouts?

In the mobile space, there is growing talk of how handset makers and carriers might be in the best position to do exactly that. Because they already have the infrastructure in place to deliver music, it makes sense for them to charge users for music—the subscription model is generally perceived as the one that would work in this scenario—and return some of those revenues to the artists.

Whether these companies will want to do the upfront work of investing in artists' recording costs is another matter. "It's very unclear who would do the investing in new artists, and how the money would be split between them, and distributors, and the artists themselves," said Kusek.

In the past, radio was the primary way that people discovered music. Now that is moving toward social networking and the word of mouth that social networking enables. "Quite a few bands have broken through as a result of word of mouth on MySpace and Facebook," said Kusek. The way Kusek envisions it, $2 would be added to your ISP or phone bill that would go into a pool to be shared by everyone involved.

A Flip-Flopped Business Model

Artists have always received royalties based on a percentage of sales of their recordings. Under the traditional model, according to Bracy, artists would then go on tour and perform live to sell more records. "Now it's almost flipped, where people are selling the records and the digital downloads to promote their tours and ability to sell merchandise," he said. "And it's unclear whether musicians will be able to shift back to gaining the majority of their revenues from recordings under any of the new business models."

Indeed, the live performance industry is booming. According to Screen Digest, a full 50% of all music revenues in 2007 came from live performances. "Look at the Stones. Look at Springsteen. They're all making a killing from their tours," said Kusek. No wonder, then, with revenues from CD sales dwindling and revenues from online downloads not adding up to significant sums, the big question—especially from newer artists' perspectives—is how to leverage technology to reap monies from a broad range of activities, not just recordings.

"Everyone is asking how digital downloads can make up for the loss in physical recordings," said eMarketer's Verna. "The far more urgent question is: How can people—whether artists or labels—monetize *all* their assets?" Kelli Richards, president and CEO of the All Access Group, an established veteran in the digital music/media arena, believes that any viable business model incorporates the full range of artist activities into the revenue stream. She is especially interested in what she calls "the concert of the future," in which savvy artists will use technology to extend their relationship with their fans in a live concert experience.

For example, prior to playing a concert in a particular location, a band could push messages to fans in an e-mail blast based on ZIP code; at the concert itself, fans could vote for the set list using their cell phones. Leaving the show, the band could send songs to fans' cell phones, send follow up e-mail messages thanking them for coming to the show, and offer them discounted merchandise that they could purchase from an online store.

27

"Concerts are the No. I category in on-demand television," pointed out Richards. "People are willing to pay top dollar for live performances, and technology is a great enabler of turning these events into opportunities to draw fans closer and generate even more revenue."

Musician Samantha Morton provides a case in point. Like most independent artists, she makes most of her money by touring. Although she does record and make the CDs available at her concerts, as well as digital downloads available through iTunes, she uses recorded music sales primarily as vehicles to promote her live appearances. Each CD she presses costs her $1.60; she routinely hands them out to fans and tells them to pay her whatever they think they are worth. Rather than the $1 she gets if one of her songs sells on iTunes, she gets an average of $10 per CD, which leaves her with a net profit of more than $8.

Digital downloads are both a discovery mechanism and advertisement for the album, just as radio used to be.

Still, she sees this less as a significant revenue stream and more as a way to increase her fan base. She encourages people to burn copies of her CDs and give them out to friends. She has even provided blank CDs to concert goers to facilitate this way of spreading the word about her music and advocates free file sharing of her music over the Internet for the same reason.

Is Online Popularity Translating to Revenue for Artists?

But is Internet popularity translating into actual revenue for artists? This is the million-dollar question. "It's very nascent, but I don't believe that sales generated on MySpace or YouTube or Facebook are adding up to very much," said Richards. Like others, she believes that online tracks will promote sales of what she calls "value-added content": backstage or behind-the-scenes footage, outtakes, interviews, or opportunities to interact with the musicians more intimately.

Faber is also a big believer in this value-added concept that piggybacks onto digital downloads. Under this scenario, the digital downloads are both a discovery mechanism and advertisement for the album, just as radio used to be. "By getting tracks out there as broadly as possible, and making them as accessible as possible, you can drive demand for the album and all the value-added content that's on there," said Faber.

Faber, who was an expert witness for Napster, calls the summer of 2000, before Napster was shut down, "the golden age of music." "I absolutely believe that Napster would have been the greatest thing to happen to the music industry. People were far more engaged than they ever were before or have been since in discovering music and passing it along to others." Indeed, surveys showed that Napster was associated with greater album purchasing, he said.

There will be the Google of the music business, and it will happen.

"Who needs major labels, and *Rolling Stone*, and MTV? You've got friends, and ways of communicating and talking about bands," said Bracy. "Hundreds of bands, not a single superstar among them, all have significant followings and fan bases thanks to technology."

The online music site Pitchfork has turned out to be incredibly influential at promoting discovery of relatively unknown bands. After a rave review on Pitchfork, Arcade Fire immediately began selling out venues all across the country, pointed out Bob Lefsetz, an independent music producer in Santa Monica and author of the Lefsetz Letter. "There will be the Google of the music business, and it *will* happen," said Lefsetz. "Someone will create the MTV, the *Rolling Stone* of the online music business—the place to go for the online filter that tells you what you need to be listening to."

"A lot of people who had lost faith in the industry are very excited about all the possibilities—the potential of finding out about new artists who have been flying under the radar," said Verna. "Clearly, there's terrific music out there, it's online, and an open field for companies to develop really great technology for filtering through the drek and finding the gold, and getting people to actually pay money for it."

4

Retail Music Stores Must Adapt to the Changing Music Industry

Hil Anderson

Hil Anderson is a writer for United Press International.

Because of the digital music revolution of the last several years, the days of brick-and-mortar retail music stores are numbered. As a solution to the major decrease in record sales, a consortium of six well-known record store chains has launched Echo, a joint venture aimed at catering to a growing segment of music fans that download their music from the Internet. The partner companies believe they have an edge over traditional record labels because they can sell music from multiple sources. Jerry Comstock, chief executive officer of Wherehouse Music, one of Echo's partners believes that, "Retail has always been about more than simply selling CDs." And with the direction the music industry is headed, it looks like it is going to have to be.

T he retail side of the music business announced a joint venture Monday that will seek to carve out a major role for itself in the growing market for online downloads of popular recordings.

Faced with sagging CD sales over the past two years, a consortium of six well-known record store chains launched Echo, a joint venture aimed at catering to the growing download market in a manner that complements their network of traditional brick-and-mortar record stores.

Hil Anderson, "Record Retailers Join Music Download Fray," *United Press International*, January 28, 2003. Reproduced by permission.

"Echo was established to create a viable business strategy that combines physical and digital music distribution," explained Dan Hart, CEO of the new Los Angeles-based enterprise. "Music retailers can utilize their long history and expertise in building customer relationships, marketing music and breaking new artists in order to provide a digital music experience that truly serves the consumer."

The New Digital Music Experience

The digital music experience envisioned by Echo is one in which music is licensed and sold over the Internet; however, the six individual chains will be able to price and advertise music as they see fit.

"This will, for the first time, bring real competition to the digital music marketplace," Alan Malasky, Echo's anti-trust attorney, said in a press release.

Echo's six partners each hold an equal stake in the venture. They include Tower Records, Wherehouse Music, Virgin, FYE Stores, Hastings Entertainment and Best Buy.

Echo is not the first attempt by mainstream music companies to crack the digital market that grew up around Napster, the renegade file-sharing Web site that literally allowed millions of users worldwide to sort through and download songs stashed in MP3 computer files free of charge.

Retail has always been about more than simply selling CDs.

While wildly popular with a generally youthful and cash-poor audience of computer-savvy music fans, Napster became the bane of the established recording industry. The company was knocked out of commission last year by the recording industry, which successfully argued in federal court that Napster was abetting record piracy and cheating companies and musicians out of their rightful royalties under copyright law.

Filling the Napster Void

New file-sharing technologies have popped up to fill the Napster void, while the music industry has found limited success in its own attempts to market its wares online.

The companies that own Echo believe that they can succeed where the record labels struggled in their attempts to market downloads because they have name recognition and the ability to sell products from multiple labels. They will also be able to offer in-store specials and the technological means of downloading music into customers' personal MP3 players in the store.

"Retail has always been about more than simply selling CDs," said Jerry Comstock, chief executive officer of Wherehouse Music. "We are in the customer relationship business."

Wherehouse earlier this month filed for bankruptcy protection, attributing a 15-percent decline in sales to online piracy and increasing competition from discount retail outlets.

Blunting the Piracy Problem

Although the record labels have yet to be approached about granting licenses, it is expected that they will quickly agree since Echo offers them a means of blunting the piracy problem while at the same time giving them a digital relationship with the record store chains that now sell the lion's share of their CDs.

Any opportunity retailers have to find additional revenue in a time of falling sales is a positive.

Some analysts have cautioned that digital retailing depends to a large extent on the price offered to online devotees who are unwilling to pay $15 or more for a CD, however would be drawn to the selection and stability of a familiar brand name.

"Any opportunity retailers have to find additional revenue in a time of falling sales is a positive," Michael Nathanson, an analyst at Sanford C. Bernstein, told The New York Times. "We continue to think that pricing has to come down to get pirates off the free sites and onto legitimate ones."

The Sound Quality of Music Is at Risk in the Music Industry

Suhas Sreedhar

Suhas Sreedhar is assistant director of the Center for Scientific Writings at Stevens Institute of Technology.

Recorded music that sounds louder on average, rather than exhibiting more dynamic range, gets more attention from listeners. This set off a "loudness war" between record companies, which began in the vinyl-record era. However, the advent of the compact disc (CD) removed the limitations of analog recordings. Recorded music has become louder and louder over the last two decades, at the cost of the dynamic range or, essentially, the quality of recordings. Furthermore, the loudness of today's recorded music actually fatigues listeners and raises the risk of hearing loss. As a result, the continuing loudness war and customers' lack of awareness of—or indifference to—sound quality compromises recorded music now and, potentially, in the future.

You're listening to your favorite Pink Floyd CD on your home stereo when you accidentally hit the "change CD" button on the control panel. All goes quiet for a bit as your CD player urgently shifts to play whatever is in the next tray. With dread, you desperately reach for the volume knob, but it's too late—your speakers blast the latest Green Day album. Reacting like you were just pricked by a pin, your hand jolts

Suhas Sreedhar, "The Future of Music," *IEEE Spectrum Online*, August 2007. http:// spectrum.ieee.org. Reproduced by permission.

to the volume knob and turns it down. You breathe a sigh of relief. But that's not the end of it. Ten minutes later you feel that something isn't right. Even though you love this album, you can't listen to it anymore. You shut it off, tired, puzzled, and confused. This always seems to happen when you switch from a classic album to a modern one. What you've just experienced is something called overcompression of the dynamic range. Welcome to the loudness war.

The loudness war, what many audiophiles refer to as an assault on music (and ears), has been an open secret of the recording industry for nearly the past two decades and has garnered more attention in recent years as CDs have pushed the limits of loudness thanks to advances in digital technology. The "war" refers to the competition among record companies to make louder and louder albums. But the loudness war could be doing more than simply pumping up the volume and angering aficionados—it could be responsible for halting technological advances in sound quality for years to come.

Overcompression

The smoking gun of the loudness war is the difference between the waveforms of songs 20 years ago and now. . . .

Music, like speech, is dynamic. There are quiet and loud moments that serve to accentuate each other and convey meaning by their relative levels of loudness. For instance, if someone is talking and suddenly shouts, the loudness of the shout, in addition to the content, conveys a message—be it a sense of urgency, surprise, or anger.

When the dynamic range of a song is heavily reduced for the sake of achieving loudness, the sound becomes analogous to someone constantly shouting everything he or she says. Not only is all impact lost, but the constant level of the sound is fatiguing to the ear. So why is achieving greater and greater loudness so important that the natural ebb and flow of music has been so readily sacrificed?

The answer goes back to the beginnings of recorded music.

The Vinyl Era

Loudness has always been a desirable quality for mainstream popular music. The louder a song is overall, the more it stands out from ambient noise and the more it grabs your attention. Studies in the field of psychoacoustics, which investigates how humans perceive sound, show that people judge how loud a sound is based on its average loudness, not its peak loudness. So even though there might be two songs whose loudest parts reach the same loudness level in decibels (dB), the one with the higher average level is generally perceived as louder.

As far back as the early 1960s, record companies began engaging in a loudness battle when they observed that louder songs in jukeboxes tended to garner more attention than quieter ones. To maintain their competitive edge, record companies wanted to keep raising the loudness of their songs. But the physical properties of vinyl records limited engineers' ability to perpetually increase loudness.

A vinyl record consists of a lacquer into which small V-shaped grooves—vibrational transcriptions of analog sound—are cut. Creating a record in the studio involves a process called mastering, where songs are sonically adjusted and placed into an appropriate order to fit the given medium's requirements. Mastering for vinyl was always a balance between loudness and playing time. The louder you wanted a song to be, the wider the groove needed to be in order to accommodate the larger amplitude of the transcription. Since there's only a limited amount of usable surface area per vinyl disc, gaining loudness meant sacrificing playing time, especially on a long playing (LP) record where upwards of six songs were often fit on each side of the disc.

In order to save the cost of manufacturing an excessive number of vinyl discs per album, playing time usually won out over loudness. Live music typically has a dynamic range of 120 dB, peaking at about the same loudness of a jet engine (though some concerts have gone even louder). Vinyl records tend to have about 70 dB of dynamic range. This meant that in order to fit a song onto a record, it either needed to have its overall amplitude reduced or it needed to be compressed— have its peaks brought down to a lower level—to fit within the given range. How much of each was done varied from record to record and defined the art of mastering. However, the tools of analog signal processing limited the amount of compression that was possible.

The invention of digital audio and the compact disc became a new fuel for a previously existing loudness race.

Analog compressors of this era were basically voltage control amplifiers that varied the level of an output signal based on a control voltage, similar to the devices that regulate signals in AM radio. Such compressors were typically used on individual instrument tracks (vocals, guitar, etc.) to add clarity to a sound or to change the sound of an instrument for effect. However, in some cases, such as with the hit singles put out by Motown Records (for example, "Want Ads" by Honey Cone), compressors were used to boost the loudness of songs to higher-than-average levels. Mastering engineers accomplished this by reducing the dynamic range of a song so that the entire song could be amplified to a greater extent before it pushed the physical limits of the medium. This became known as "hot" mastering and was typically done on singles where each side of the record only contained one song. Generally, however, the average level of songs and albums stayed relatively the same throughout the period.

"CD" Behavior

"The invention of digital audio and the compact disc became a new fuel for a previously existing loudness race," says Bob Katz, a renowned mastering engineer and one of the first outspoken critics of dynamic-range overcompression. "The reason is that the analog media did not permit what we would call 'normalization' to the peak level."

When the compact disc (CD) was introduced in the early 1980s, there was much for audiophiles to be happy about. Digital audio removed many of the physical restrictions vinyl had imposed, such as concerns about surface noise (caused by dust, scratches, the lacquer itself, and so on) and limited dynamic range. The CD was capable of supporting a dynamic range of about 96 dB. For most of the 1980s, when CDs were still high-end products and mastering engineers largely did not have access to digital signal-processing technologies, albums released on CD tended to make use of this better dynamic range.

Unlike vinyl, which had varying loudness limits due to its physical characteristics, the CD had a definitive peak loudness limit due to its specified digitizing standard, a form of pulse code modulation (PCM). PCM had previously been used in telephony as a method of digitizing an analog signal. When an analog signal is sampled for digitization, each level of the signal is quantized (stored as a number in binary). How frequently samples of the signal are taken is specified by the sampling rate, and the total number of unique quantization levels capable of being stored is determined by the number of bits. When Sony and Philips specified the standard for CD audio, they determined that the sampling rate would be 44.1 kHz with 16 bits per sample. Using the rule of thumb, the approximation of 6.02 dB of dynamic range per bit gave CD audio roughly 96 dB of dynamic range. The highest loudness level (16 bits of all 1's) was designated as 0 decibels full scale (dBFS). Lower levels were assigned negative numbers.

In the 1980s, CDs were mastered so that songs generally peaked at about −6 dBFS with their root mean square (RMS)—or average levels—hovering around −20 dBFS to −18 dBFS. As multidisc CD changers began to gain prominence in households toward the end of the decade, the same jukebox-type loudness competition started all over again as record companies wanted their CDs to stick out more than their competitors'. By the end of the 1980s, songs on CDs were amplified to the point where their peaks started pushing the loudness limit of 0 dBFS. At this point, the only way to raise the average levels of songs without having their loudest parts clipped—the digital equivalent of distortion, where information is lost because it exceeds the bit capacity—was to compress the peaks.

While analog compressors had been limited in the extent to which they could reduce peak levels, digital compressors were much more powerful. As mastering engineers began to get hold of digital signal-processing tools, they were able to "hot" master songs even more. The process was similar to what had been done on some vinyl singles—peak levels were brought down by a certain amount, and then the entire waveform was amplified until the (now reduced) peaks once again reached 0 dBFS. The result? The average level of the entire song increased.

The 1990s saw average amplitude levels go from around −15 dBFS to as much as −6 dBFS in extreme cases. Most songs in this decade, however, remained at around −12 dBFS. The 2000s saw the loudness war reach its height, with most current songs having an average level of −9 dBFS or higher. From the mid 1980s to now, the average loudness of CDs increased by a factor of 10, and the peaks of songs are now one-tenth of what they used to be. The loudness war is also not just confined to the big four record companies (Warner Music Group, EMI, Sony BMG, and Universal Music Group). Over-compression is now widespread and performed by independent labels and international record companies.

The CD Is Dead; Loudness Continues

The biggest change from 15 years ago to today is how people consume music. With more than 100 million iPods sold world-wide as of early this year [2007], more and more people are listening to music on the go rather than at their home stereos. Physical media like CDs are on their way out. And yet over-compression continues to plague the music world.

Even though the CD might be in its death throes, most digital music available online was mastered for CDs. Popular formats like MP3, AAC, and Free Lossless Audio Codec (FLAC) merely use data-compression techniques (not to be confused with dynamic-range compression) to reduce the amount of data a song encoded in PCM takes up. As long as the specter of CDs continues to haunt the online world, down-loaded songs will still be subject to overcompression.

Many listeners have subconsciously felt the effects of overcompressed songs in the form of auditory fatigue, where it actually becomes tiring to continue listening to the music.

But the problem doesn't just lie on the production end. If people are listening to songs in a noisy environment—such as in their cars, on trains, in airport waiting rooms, at work, or in a dormitory—the music needs to be louder to compensate. Dynamic-range compression does just that and more. Not only does it raise the average loudness of the song, but by do-ing so it eliminates all the quiet moments of a song as well. So listeners are now able to hear the entire song above the noise without getting frustrated by any inaudible low parts.

This might be one of the biggest reasons why most people are completely unaware of the loss of dynamics in modern music. They are listening to songs in less-than-ideal environments on a constant basis. But many listeners have subconsciously felt the effects of overcompressed songs in the form of auditory fatigue, where it actually becomes tiring to continue listening to the music.

"You want music that breathes. If the music has stopped breathing, and it's a continuous wall of sound, that will be fatiguing," says Katz. "If you listen to it loudly as well, it will potentially damage your ears before the older music did because the older music had room to breathe."

Some audiophiles find relief by going back to the past. A few musicians still continue to release their albums on vinyl records (in addition to CDs and online formats). Because vinyl cannot support the loudness that CDs can, these modern vinyl releases are much quieter than their CD counterparts. But they are often less compressed as well, and, in some instances, remastered in a way that is as dynamic as albums released in the 1960s and 1970s.

One of the most prominent examples of this is the recent Red Hot Chili Peppers album Stadium Arcadium, which was remastered for vinyl by mastering engineer Steve Hoffman with the intent of providing full dynamic sound. Hoffman is one of the few mastering engineers who have actually refused to take certain jobs because he's been asked to overcompress music. "[It happens] all the time," says Hoffman. "At least once a week."

But turning to vinyl for uncompressed music might not always provide salvation. In order to save the cost of remastering, record companies might simply take the compressed master of a song, reduce the overall loudness, and place it on vinyl. Katz warns, "You could take the Red Hot Chili Peppers recording and put it onto vinyl just as it came from CD, and it would sound just as fatiguing. [The only difference is] you'd just have to turn the volume control up because you couldn't get the peak level the same."

Tearing Down the Wall

Audiophiles looking to the future for relief from overcompression see a cloudy picture. DVD-Audio and Super Audio Compact Disc (SACD) are two high-fidelity formats that were thought to be solutions to the loudness war. Both formats offer not only a greater dynamic range than CD but also higher sampling rates. This allows for frequencies higher than what most humans are capable of hearing to be encoded onto the medium, addressing a common complaint by people who prefer analog over digital because they claim they can hear these frequencies.

DVD-Audio uses PCM encoding that can support 24-bit, 192 kHz stereo sound (contrasted with the CD's 16 bit, 44.1 kHz) yielding 144 dB of dynamic range, 14 dB over the human threshold of pain. SACD, like the CD, was developed by Sony and Philips and uses a form of pulse-density modulation (PDM) encoding branded as Direct Stream Digital. Basically, instead of having 16-bit samples at a frequency of 44.1 kHz, it takes 1-bit samples at 64 times that rate (2.82 MHz). It has a dynamic range of about 120 dB. Additionally, both SACD and DVD-Audio are capable of high-fidelity five-channel surround sound.

Since their introduction in 2000, however, neither format has taken hold. An overwhelming majority of releases have been of the classical music genre, which has generally not been subject to overcompression to begin with. So even if audiophiles wanted to spend upward of $300 for a DVD-Audio or SACD player, chances are they won't be able to buy their favorite popular albums in either medium.

Since music has gone online, the possibility of having high-fidelity digital files remains, and formats such as FLAC are capable of supporting 24-bit audio. Slim Devices, a company acquired last year by Logitech, has created two products—the Squeezebox and the Transporter—that wirelessly stream digital files from a computer or the Internet to high-end stereo receivers. Both are capable of handling 24-bit audio, but the problem, says Sean Adams, former CEO of Slim Devices, is lack of content.

If record companies aren't making use of the full dynamic capability of CDs, then why bother moving to another format with even more potentially unused capability?

"If we're going to go to higher levels of sound quality, the real problem is actually getting the content out. Right now, unfortunately, the industry has kind of gone backward from CD quality. When MP3 came out, [it was called] CD quality when it really wasn't," says Adams. "We've made some improvements since then with better [compression techniques], but it's really a function of people demanding better sound quality. That has to happen first before the [recording] industry's going to start producing it."

Overcompression, however, seems to be one of the biggest obstacles to overcome. With music being compressed to have smaller and smaller dynamic ranges, the need for the next high-fidelity audio format vanishes. If record companies aren't making use of the full dynamic capability of CDs, then why bother moving to another format with even more potentially unused capability? And with the average consumer being either completely unaware of, or only subconsciously irritated by, the current state of overcompressed music, there is little incentive for sound quality to progress. Consequently, all the potential benefits of higher-quality audio—lifelike dynamic range, greater frequency response, and multichannel surround sound—remain unseen, even though the technology exists today. Audiophiles are forced to return to vinyl and analog recordings that should have been obsolete 20 years ago.

But there might still be hope for getting out of the loudness war. RMS (average) normalization algorithms, such as Replay Gain, have been implemented in many digital audio players and work to bring all songs in a digital library to the same average level. With Replay Gain enabled, songs originating from many CDs are processed and played back at a consistent average level of loudness. This helps listeners because they no longer have to adjust their volume each time they go from one album to another. And while such normalization cannot undo the compression of music (it amplifies or reduces the song in its entirety), it counteracts any efforts that were put in to make one song louder than another, essentially nullifying the loudness war altogether.

Many hope that widespread implementation of technologies like Replay Gain will make record companies see that further and further compression in the name of competitive loudness is a feckless task, and slowly but surely popular music will begin to return to a dynamic, less-compressed state. In fact, many digital audio players have caught on; Winamp uses Replay Gain, and iTunes has its own normalization option called Sound Check, which also works on iPods.

Whether the loudness war can end and give rise to the next generation of high-fidelity audio depends heavily on the attitudes of consumers. Unlike the CD and DVD video, there is no overwhelming industrial push toward the next level of sound quality. How songs and albums will sound will depend entirely on whether or not the listener actually cares about the intricacies of the music.

6

The CD Is Obsolete

Daniel B. Wood

Daniel B. Wood is a staff writer for The Christian Science Monitor.

The growth of the online music industry has led to the decline of compact disc (CD) sales and has been replaced by pay-per-track services or subscription music businesses. Even though it is illegal to download music on the Internet free of charge, there is a proliferation of file-exchanging services on the web that also have contributed to the demise of CDs. Some worry that the way music is now exchanged will continue to undermine the single-concept album such as the Beatles' Sgt. Pepper's Lonely Hearts Club Band, *but others think that the ease of the Internet will better equip fans to share albums with each other. The only thing that is certain is that the future of the music industry is under attack from all sides and must reinvent itself to survive.*

As he paws through compact discs in Borders Bookstore here, dentist Seth Kinder's eyes widen. "$18.99 for one CD with 10 songs?" he says, reading the price tag on Leonard Cohen's "Ten New Songs." "I can join an online service for two months for that and have unlimited access to 180,000 songs."

Mr. Kinder's impulse to go to the Internet and pull down whatever music he wants—one song at a time and with far less impact on his wallet—signals one of the biggest changes to hit the music industry since the LP.

For years, millions of Americans swapped songs on the Web free of charge. But then the courts stepped in and shut down the popular online music service, Napster, that was used to download the songs and became the nemesis of the music industry.

The End of CDs

Now, however, a growing number of record companies themselves are offering songs over the Internet for a modest fee. Stung by the continued availability of free music from "pirate" companies operating since Napster, they're offering subscription services that allow consumers to buy songs one at a time online.

The hard copy, album-form compact disc will die. It is happening.

The move is ushering in a fundamental change in how music is conceived and sold. It may also lead to the eventual demise of the multi-song album or CD format itself.

"The hard copy, album-form compact disc will die. It is happening," says Don Gorter, chair of the Music Business Department at Berklee College of Music in Boston. "The manner and length in which artists make their musical statements will likely look far different than today."

The latest companies to succumb to the forces of the Web were Universal Music Group and Sony Entertainment, two of the world's largest record companies. Earlier this month, they combined forces to help make it easier and cheaper for consumers to buy songs on the Internet.

They join eight other new licensing and selling services that now include participation from all five of the world's leading record companies. The new subscription services have come in the wake of worldwide piracy that is costing the industry billions a year, threatening the decades-old economic structure of the music business.

"The recording industry as we know it is under attack from all sides and trying to figure out how to reinvent itself," says Drew Borst, an analyst for Bernstein & Company in New York.

The Changing Music Industry

With their eyes on such an uncertain future, many artists are pulling back and waiting to see how new models of business pan out. Country star Clint Black recently laid out a detailed plan to completely circumvent record companies—with individual units purchased via the Internet from his own website, clintblack.com.

How quickly this new world plays out depends on the changing behavior of two distinct cohorts of consumers, as well as the interplay between them. One of the two groups is younger buyers, aged 16-24, who have little incentive to purchase music because of the proliferation of free (if illegal), file-exchanging services.

While offering a fee-based alternative to absolutely free music seems ludicrous and futile to some, the new services are attracting significant numbers of subscribers.

"Why in heaven's name would I subscribe to a subscription service for $10 to $25 a month for access to a limited number of songs, when I can have practically any song that exists for free?" asks Carey Brooks, a teenager in Sherman Oaks who has downloaded about 500 songs free from an online swapping service known as Morpheus.

From her computer hard drive, Brooks and others then download the digitized songs into other formats, from portable MP3 players, to tape decks, to CDs. While offering a fee-based alternative to absolutely free music seems ludicrous and futile to some, the new services are attracting significant numbers of subscribers, company officials say.

"A year ago, most people were telling us subscription services were a pipe dream—now nine are up and running with pretty good success," says Michael Graves, a spokesman for Lycos Rhapsody. The service, offered at Listen.com, boasts 185,000 titles via a number of packages for prices ranging from about $10 to $25 per month.

And some analysts say the prospect of sophisticated future services may appeal to older buyers.

"Downloading and organizing free music is fine when you have hours to spend doing it, but what about when you work all day and don't want to mess with all that," says Mr. Graves. "Consumers will think $10 a month to end that hassle is a small price to pay."

The Effects of File Sharing

How such buying patterns play out may also continue to undermine the single-concept, album CD such as the Beatles' *Sgt. Pepper's Lonely Hearts Club Band,* Pink Floyd's *Dark Side of the Moon,* and Bruce Springsteen's *The River.*

But the music industry is hoping that their online services, too, will be able to cater to those who want to dim the lights, switch on a lava lamp, and take in an uninterrupted Pink Floyd album in its entirety through the Internet. Unlike free services, record companies say their services allow for faster and easier ways to download collections of songs (including albums). They also tout the sound quality of files; the ability to list tracks and organize songs by artist, album, or title; and the inclusion of features such as Internet radio.

But the success of the music subscription services may also depend on record companies cracking down on university computer systems that engage in large amounts of illegal file-sharing. Companies are expected to increase an activity known as "spoofing" in which they flood the Internet with empty or spoiled files as a way to thwart illegal swapping. And they hope good old-fashioned consciousness raising among consumers will help.

"We need to educate a whole generation about the real costs of illegal file-sharing," says Graves. "Most parents wouldn't let their kids go shoplifting. Yet they go out and buy [CD burning] technology that allows their kids to shoplift via the Internet."

Whereas many observers both inside and outside the recording industry have long held a Chicken Little ("sky is falling") view of the current pressures on the music business, more now are taking a sanguine view that the industry had it coming by not catering to what consumers want.

But the all-of-the-above cage rattling is music to the ears of consumers like Kinder, who says he does more than buy music. He also played in a band during college and has visions of cutting, then selling his own CDs in the future.

"I don't see this implosion of record companies as anything near a bad thing," he says. "This is going to allow thousands of people just like myself to write their songs, record them, market, and share them with others like me and have a ball doing it."

7

The CD Is Not Obsolete

Daniel Gross

Daniel Gross is a columnist for Slate, *an online news magazine, and* Newsweek. *He is also the author of* Pop! Why Bubbles Are Great for the Economy.

Although compact disc (CD) sales have dramatically slipped in the last several years due to the rise of file-sharing and pay-per-track online music services, the CD should not be counted out just yet. Giant music retailers like Tower Records may have gone out of business, but brick-and-mortar music retailers that cater to customers with specific tastes and carry specialized selections have not been hit by the dwindling CD sales of major label artists. In addition, novelty CD sales at Starbucks locations are robust, as they are at online retailers like Amazon. It is the old methods of selling CDs that are dying off, not the CD itself—at least for a long time.

Mozart wrote only one *Requiem*, but in recent years, music journalists have written about 80 requiems for the compact disc, mostly in the key of boo-hoo major. Data from the Recording Industry Association of America show that between 2000 and 2005, the number of CDs shipped fell 25 percent to 705.4 million, while their value slipped 20 percent, from $13.2 billion to $10.5 billion. During the first six months of 2006, CD sales dropped 14 percent more. And as Ethan Smith wrote in the *Wall Street Journal* last week, CD sales are down another 20 percent in the first quarter of 2007. . . . Jeff

Leeds, writing in the *New York Times*, penned an obituary for the CD, which has been driven into oblivion by consumers' preference for digital singles over albums. Last year [in 2006], hundreds of music stores closed, among them the 89 outlets of the greatly missed Tower Records.

Conclusion: *The CD is dead!*

Except, it's not. Last Sunday, Paul de Barros of the *Seattle Times* chronicled the growth of Silver Platters, a local chain of CD stores that just took over an old Tower Records space. Meanwhile, savvy new-era businesses are jumping into the CD business. The same day Smith's piece appeared in the *Journal*, Starbucks announced its record label would issue its first CD this summer [in 2007], from Paul McCartney. Earlier this month [in March 2007], Amazon launched a classical music retail outlet, capitalizing on the genre's impressive 2006 comeback, which was driven by massive CD sales from the unholy trinity of cheesy, nonclassical classical artists: Andrea Bocelli, Josh Groban, and Il Divo.

Is the CD dying as a commercial product? Sure. But it's got a lot of dying left to do.

An Industry in Crisis

Clearly, it's trickier than ever to make, market, and sell CDs. It's an industry in crisis. But CDs are still a significant business. All the kids, and many adults, have iPods. But plenty of baby boomers still buy the shiny discs; CDs account for three-quarters of all music sold.

What we are witnessing is not so much the imminent death of CDs but the death of the old methods of selling CDs. It's still possible to make money in the CD business— any business with more than $7 billion in retail sales should allow someone, somewhere, to make a profit. The incumbents are getting killed, but upstarts are thriving, using different methods.

Legacy music retailers and manufacturers now face many of the same difficulties as American auto companies. They built a business infrastructure—national chains, huge outlets in high-profile locations, layers of management—predicated on selling massive and growing quantities of CDs for $15.99 and up. Like the American automakers, they found that new competition—from iTunes, file-sharing, and online retailers—severely cut into their margins, their market share, and their pricing power. In such an environment, companies with significant capital invested in stores and substantial overhead costs get destroyed. And as they fail, they do so loudly, inspiring widespread pessimism.

The New Rules

Yet the new rules open opportunities for upstarts who approach the business of making and marketing CDs in a fundamentally different way. Unlike fallen chains such as Tower, boutiques such as Silver Platters and Rasputin in San Francisco don't spend on expensive national advertising. They're more like art-house theaters. Since they cater more to music aficionados than to the masses who used to flood into HMV for the latest Mariah Carey CD, the demise of the blockbuster CD doesn't put a crimp in their sales.

In the age of file-sharing and iTunes, people simply aren't willing to pay $16 for a collection of songs they may not want. That proved to be fatal for Tower Records. But for Amazon.com, such price pressure doesn't really matter. The company has built up a commercial infrastructure that enables it to sell and deliver all sorts of cheap objects, from books to toys. Blogger Barry Ritholtz noted in January [2007] that most of the top-selling CDs at Amazon.com sell for *less than $10*. For Amazon, which already has huge investments in warehouses, software, and its Web site, carving out some extra space for classical CDs doesn't require a huge incremental investment. What's more, since its inception, the store has been designed to run on very low margins.

In the case of Starbucks, the economics of selling CDs are even more compelling. With its 14,000-odd outlets, the company already has a massive, highly profitable retail channel that generates immense foot traffic daily. Each store is conveniently outfitted with counters, which are ideal for stocking a variety of noncoffee products that have mass appeal: chocolates, books, and CDs. Both Barnes & Noble and Borders may be having a difficult time making money selling wide selections of books in huge retail spaces. But when Starbucks decides to stock a single book, say Mitch Albom's *For One More Day* or Ishmael Beah's *A Long Way Gone*, it can easily turn a profit on every sale. Starbucks found the same sort of success with the Ray Charles album *Genius Loves Company* in 2004. Starbucks has also invested in building its Hear Music concept, where customers can buy coffee, buy CDs, or download music, into a small chain.

Is the CD dying as a commercial product? Sure. But it's got a lot of dying left to do. And in the meantime, there's still money to be made selling discs loaded with the music of Josh Groban, Alban Berg, and Rod Stewart.

8

Vinyl Records Threaten the Future of CDs

Eliot Van Buskirk

Eliot Van Buskirk is senior editor for music at CNET, a technology-centered media company.

Though vinyl records may seem archaic in an era of MP3 players, digital downloads, and file sharing, the format is making a comeback and may hasten the extinction of the compact disc (CD). Vinyl record sales are thriving among deejays, audiophiles, and music aficionados, who claim that vinyl offers the truest listening experience because digital music formats cannot match the warm, nuanced sound of analog recordings. Also, many music consumers have MP3 versions of their vinyl records for convenience and portability, which leaves the CD further behind. So, despite what the music industry says, vinyl is back in demand, and production of vinyl records is up across all genres.

As counterintuitive as it may seem in this age of iPods and digital downloads, vinyl—the favorite physical format of indie music collectors and audiophiles—is poised to re-enter the mainstream, or at least become a major tributary.

Talk to almost anyone in the music business' vital indie and DJ scenes and you'll encounter a uniformly optimistic picture of the vinyl market.

"I'm hearing from labels and distributors that vinyl is way up," said Ian Connelly, client relations manager of independent distributor alliance IODA, in an e-mail interview. "And not just the boutique, limited-edition colored vinyl that Jesu/Isis-style fans are hot for right now."

Pressing plants are ramping up production, but where is the demand coming from? Why do so many people still love vinyl, even though its bulky, analog nature is anathema to everything music is supposed to be these days? Records, the vinyl evangelists will tell you, provide more of a connection between fans and artists. And many of today's music fans buy 180-gram vinyl LPs for home listening and MP3s for their portable devices.

"For many of us, and certainly for many of our artists, the vinyl is the true version of the release," said Matador's Patrick Amory. "The size and presence of the artwork, the division into sides, the better sound quality, above all the involvement and work the listener has to put in, all make it the format of choice for people who really care about music."

Because these music fans also listen using portable players and computers, Matador and other labels include coupons in record packaging that can be used to download MP3 versions of the songs. Amory called the coupon program "hugely popular."

The vinyl-MP3 tag team might just hasten the long-predicted death of the CD.

Vinyl's Sonic Superiority

Portability is no longer any reason to stick with CDs, and neither is audio quality. Although vinyl purists are ripe for parody, they're right about one thing: Records can sound better than CDs.

Although CDs have a wider dynamic range, mastering houses are often encouraged to compress the audio on CDs to make it as loud as possible: It's the so-called loudness war.

Since the audio on vinyl can't be compressed to such extremes, records generally offer a more nuanced sound.

Another reason for vinyl's sonic superiority is that no matter how high a sampling rate is, it can never contain all of the data present in an analog groove, Nyquist's theorem [or the sampling theorem] to the contrary.

"The digital world will never get there," said Chris Ashworth, owner of United Record Pressing, the country's largest record pressing plant.

Golden-eared audiophiles have long testified to vinyl's warmer, richer sound. And now demand for vinyl is on the rise. Pressing plants that were already at capacity are staying there, while others are cranking out more records than they did last year in order to keep pace with demand.

Don MacInnis, owner of Record Technology in Camarillo, California, predicts production will be up 25 percent over last year by the end of 2007. And he's not talking about small runs of dance music for DJs, but the whole gamut of music: "new albums, reissues, majors and indies . . . jazz, blues, classical, pop and a lot of (classic) rock."

Turntables are hot again as well. Insound, an online music retailer that recently began selling USB turntables alongside vinyl, can't keep them in stock, according to the company's director, Patrick McNamara.

And on Oct. 17 [2007], Amazon.com launched a vinyl-only section stocked with a growing collection of titles and several models of record players.

Big labels still aren't buying the vinyl comeback, but it wouldn't be the first time the industry failed to identify a new trend in the music biz.

"Our numbers, at least, don't really point to a resurgence," said Jonathan Lamy, the Recording Industry Association of America's [RIAA] director of communications. Likewise,

Nielsen SoundScan, which registered a slight increase in vinyl sales last year, nonetheless showed a 43 percent decrease between 2000 and 2006.

But when it comes to vinyl, these organizations don't really know what they're talking about. The RIAA's numbers are misleading because its member labels are only now beginning to react to the growing demand for vinyl. As for SoundScan, its numbers don't include many of the small indie and dance shops where records are sold. More importantly, neither organization tracks used records sold at stores or on eBay—arguably the central clearinghouse for vinyl worldwide.

Vinyl's popularity has been underreported before.

"The Consumer Electronics Association said that only 100,000 turntables were sold in 2004. Numark alone sold more than that to pro DJs that year," said Chris Roman, product manager for Numark.

And the vinyl-MP3 tag team might just hasten the long-predicted death of the CD.

San Francisco indie band The Society of Rockets, for example, plans to release its next album strictly on vinyl and as MP3 files.

"Having just gone through the process of mastering our new album for digital and for vinyl, I can say it is completely amazing how different they really sound," said lead singer and guitarist Joshua Babcock in an e-mail interview. "The way the vinyl is so much better and warmer and more interesting to listen to is a wonder."

9

Illegal File Sharing Threatens the Future of the Music Industry

Recording Industry Association of America

Recording Industry Association of America (RIAA) is the trade group that represents the U.S. recording industry.

The unauthorized sharing of MP3s and other copyrighted digital music files is piracy. It amounts to stealing music and copyright infringement. This includes uploading and downloading copyrighted music through peer-to-peer (P2P) services, making and giving away copies of albums on compact disc (CD), and even e-mailing MP3s to your friends without the permission of the copyright holders. Because of the serious nature of these crimes, those who engage in illegal file-sharing and are found guilty may face huge fines and possible time in prison. Technology today may make it easy—and tempting—to share and get music for free, but it is illegal and harms the music industry.

Copyright law protects the value of creative work. When you make illegal copies of someone's creative work, you are stealing and breaking the law.

Most likely, you've seen the FBI warning on a movie DVD or VHS cassette—well, the same applies, with equal force, to music. If you have been illegally reproducing or distributing copyrighted music, maybe you should give it a closer read.

Federal law provides severe civil and criminal penalties for the unauthorized reproduction, distribution, rental or digital

Recording Industry Association of America, "Piracy: Online and On the Street," riaa.com, 2008. Reproduced by permission.

transmission of copyrighted sound recordings. The FBI investigates allegations of criminal copyright infringement and violators will be prosecuted.

You won't find these messages on music you've downloaded illegally, but the full weight of the law applies just the same.

The courts have consistently ruled that P2P and other unauthorized uploading and downloading inherently amount to copyright infringement and therefore constitute a crime.

So you really should find out:

- What the law says and what it means.

- How you could be breaking the law.

- How severe the penalties can be.

- What the courts say.

- What's okay . . . and what's not.

What the Law Says and What It Means

If you make unauthorized copies of copyrighted music recordings, you're stealing. You're breaking the law, and you could be held legally liable for thousands of dollars in damages.

That's pretty important information to have, considering how serious it would be if you were caught and prosecuted by the authorities or sued in civil court. It's even more important that you understand that when you illicitly make or distribute recordings, you are taking something of value from the owner without his or her permission.

You may find this surprising. After all, when you're on the Internet, digital information can seem to be as free as air. But the fact is that U.S. copyright law prohibits the unauthorized duplication, performance or distribution of a creative work.

That means you need the permission of the copyright holder before you copy and/or distribute a copyrighted music recording.

What the Courts Have to Say

For all the public confusion, a long series of court rulings has made it very clear that it's against the law both to upload and download copyrighted music without permission.

It doesn't matter whether you're dealing with sound recordings, pictures, software or written text. The courts have consistently ruled that P2P [peer-to-peer] and other unauthorized uploading and downloading inherently amount to copyright infringement and therefore constitute a crime.

If you make digital copies of copyrighted music on your computer available to anyone through the Internet without the permission of the copyright holder, you're stealing.

Don't you have a better way to spend five years and $250,000?

Examples of easy ways you could violate the law:

- Somebody you don't even know e-mails you a copy of a copyrighted song and then you turn around and e-mail copies to all of your friends.

- You make an MP3 copy of a song because the CD you bought expressly permits you to do so. But then you put your MP3 copy on the Internet, using a file-sharing network, so that millions of other people can download it.

- Even if you don't illegally offer recordings to others, you join a file-sharing network and download unauthorized copies of all the copyrighted music you want for free from the computers of other network members.

- In order to gain access to copyrighted music on the computers of other network members, you pay a fee to join a file-sharing network that isn't authorized to distribute or make copies of copyrighted music. Then you download unauthorized copies of all the music you want.

- You transfer copyrighted music using an instant messenging service.

- You have a computer with a CD burner, which you use to burn copies of music you have downloaded onto writable CDs for all of your friends.

Do the Crime, Do the Time

If you do not have legal permission, and you go ahead and copy or distribute copyrighted music anyway, you can be prosecuted in criminal court and/or sued for damages in civil court.

- Criminal penalties for first-time offenders can be as high as five years in prison and $250,000 in fines.

- Civil penalties can run into many thousands of dollars in damages and legal fees. The minimum penalty is $750 per song.

The "No Electronic Theft Law" (NET Act) is similar on copyright violations that involve digital recordings:

- Criminal penalties can run up to 5 years in prison and/or $250,000 in fines, even if you didn't do it for monetary or financial or commercial gain.

- If you did expect something in return, even if it just involves swapping your files for someone else's, as in MP3 trading, you can be sentenced to as much as 5 years in prison.

- Regardless of whether you expected to profit, you're still liable in civil court for damages and lost profits of the copyright holder.

- Or the copyright holders can sue you for up to $150,000 in statutory damages for each of their copyrighted works that you illegally copy or distribute.

If you make digital copies of copyrighted music on your computer available to anyone through the Internet without the permission of the copyright holder, you're stealing. And if you allow a P2P file-sharing network to use part of your computer's hard drive to store copyrighted recordings that anyone can access and download, you're on the wrong side of the law.

Having the hardware to make unauthorized music recordings doesn't give you the right to steal. Music has value for the artist and for everyone who works in the industry. Please respect that.

The Courts on Illegal Uploading, Downloading, and Copyrighted Sound Recordings

"As stated by Record Company Plaintiffs in their brief, 'Aimster predicates its entire service upon furnishing a "road map" for users to find, copy, and distribute copyrighted music.' . . . We agree. Defendants [Aimster] manage to do everything but actually steal the music off the store shelf and hand it to Aimster's users." *Aimster Copyright Litigation. 01-C-8933, MDL # 1425 (Memorandum Opinion and Order, September 4, 2002).*

". . . they [Aimster] apparently believe that the ongoing, massive, and unauthorized distribution and copying of Record

Company Plaintiffs' copyrighted works by Aimster's end users somehow constitutes 'personal use.' This contention is specious and unsupported by the very case on which Defendants rely." *Aimster Copyright Litigation. 01-C-8933, MDL # 1425 (Memorandum Opinion and Order, September 4, 2002).*

"Napster users infringe at least two of the copyright holders' exclusive rights. . . . Napster users who upload file names to the search index for others to copy violate plaintiffs' distribution rights. Napster users who download files containing copyrighted music violate plaintiffs' reproduction rights. . . . Virtually all Napster users engage in the unauthorized downloading or uploading of copyrighted music. . ." *A & M Records v. Napster, Inc., 239 F.3d 1004 (9th Cir. 2001).*

"Although defendant [MP3.com] seeks to portray its service as the 'functional equivalent' of storing its subscribers' CDs, in actuality defendant is re-playing for the subscribers converted versions of the recording it copied, without authorization, from plaintiffs' copyrighted CDs. On its face, this makes out a presumptive case of infringement under the Copyright Act. . . ." *UMG Recordings, Inc. v. MP3. com, Inc., 92 F. Supp. 2d 349 (S.D.N.Y. 2000).*

The Courts on Copyrighted Images

"Distributing unlawful copies of a copyrighted work violates the copyright owner's distribution right and, as a result, constitutes copyright infringement. . . . [Unlawful distribution occurs where] [f]iles of [copyrighted] information are stored in the central system, and subscribers may either 'download' information into their [computers] or 'upload' information from their home units into the central files. . . ." *Playboy Enterprises v. Russ Hardenburgh, Inc., 982 F. Supp. 503 (N.D. Ohio 1997).*

"[The Copyright Act] provides that an owner of a copyrighted work has the exclusive right to reproduce the work in copies . . . [and] to distribute copies of the work to the public. . . . Anyone who violates any of the exclusive rights of the copyright owner . . . is an infringer of the copyright." *Playboy Enterprises v. Webbworld Inc., 991 F. Supp. 543 (N.D. Tex. 1997).*

The Courts on Copyrighted Software

"Uploading is copying. Downloading is also copying. Unauthorized copying is an unauthorized use that is governed by the copyright laws. Therefore, unauthorized uploading and unauthorized downloading are unauthorized uses governed by the copyright laws. . . ." *Ohio v. Perry, 83 Ohio St. 3d 41, 697 N.E. 2d 624 (Ohio 1998).*

"The unauthorized copying of copyrighted computer programs is . . . an infringement of the copyright. . . . Unauthorized copies . . . are made when such games are uploaded to the BBS [bulletin board service] . . . [and] when they are downloaded to make additional copies by users. . . ." *Sega Enterprises v. MAPHIA, 857 F. Supp. 679 (N.D. Cal. 1994).*

By doing the right thing, you'll be doing your part to make sure that the music keeps coming.

The Courts on Copyrighted Text

"'Copying,' for the purposes of copyright law, occurs when a computer program is transferred from a permanent storage device to a computer's random access memory. In this case, copies were made when the Sega game files were uploaded to or downloaded from [the defendant's] BBS [bulletin board service]." *Sega Enterprises. v. Sabella, 1996 U.S. Dist. LEXIS 20470 (N.D. Cal. 1996).*

"Defendant Free Republic is a 'bulletin board' website whose members use the site to post news articles to which they add remarks or commentary. . . . The Plaintiffs' [Los Angeles Times and Washington Post] complaint alleges that unauthorized copying and posting of the articles on the Free Republic site constitutes copyright infringement. . . . Plaintiffs' motion for summary adjudication with respect to fair use is granted. . . ." *L.A. Times v. Free Republic, 2000 U.S. Dist. LEXIS 5669 (C.D. Cal 2000).*

"When a person browses a website, and by so doing displays the [copyrighted] Handbook, a copy of the Handbook is made in the computer's random access memory (RAM), to permit viewing of the material. And in making a copy, even a temporary one, the person who browsed infringes the copyright. Additionally, a person making a printout or reposting a copy of the Handbook on another website would infringe plaintiffs' copyright." *Intellectual Reserve, Inc. v. Utah Lighthouse Ministry, Inc., 75 F. Supp. 2d 1290 (D. Utah 1999).*

Copying Music: What's Okay . . . and What's Not

Technology has made digital copying easier than ever. But just because advances in technology make it possible to copy music doesn't mean it's legal to do so. Here are tips from some record labels on how to enjoy the music while respecting rights of others in the digital world. Stick with these, and you'll be doing right by the people who created the music.

Internet Copying

- It's okay to download music from sites authorized by the owners of the copyrighted music, whether or not such sites charge a fee.

- It's never okay to download unauthorized music from pirate sites (web or FTP [file transfer protocol]) or peer-to-peer systems. Examples of peer-to-peer systems making unauthorized music available for download include: Kazaa, Grokster, WinMX, LimeWire, Bearshare, Aimster, Morpheus, and Gnutella.

- It's never okay to make unauthorized copies of music available to others (that is, uploading music) on peer-to-peer systems.

Copying CDs

- It's okay to copy music onto an analog cassette, but not for commercial purposes.

- It's also okay to copy music onto special audio CD-Rs, mini-discs, and digital tapes (because royalties have been paid on them)—but, again, not for commercial purposes.

- Beyond that, there's no legal "right" to copy the copyrighted music on a CD onto a CD-R. However, burning a copy of CD onto a CD-R, or transferring a copy onto your computer hard drive or your portable music player, won't usually raise concerns so long as:

  - The copy is made from an authorized original CD that you legitimately own.

  - The copy is just for your personal use. It's not a personal use—in fact, it's illegal—to give away the copy or lend it to others for copying.

- The owners of copyrighted music have the right to use protection technology to allow or prevent copying.

- Remember, it's never okay to sell or make commercial use of a copy that you make.

Are there occasionally exceptions to these rules? Sure. A "garage" or unsigned band might want you to download its own music; but, bands that own their own music are free to make it available legally by licensing it. And, remember that there are lots of authorized sites where music can be downloaded for free. Better to be safe than sorry—don't assume that downloading or burning is legal just because technology makes it easy to do so.

Enjoy the music. By doing the right thing, you'll be doing your part to make sure that the music keeps coming.

10

Illegal File Sharing Enhances the Future of the Music Industry

Sean Silverthorne

Sean Silverthorne is editor of HBS Working Knowledge, *the publication for Harvard Business School.*

Contrary to the alarming claims of the music industry, illegal peer-to-peer (P2P) file-sharing can actually boost compact disc (CD) sales. For example, research shows that a major segment of file-sharers, or "samplers," usually purchase an album on CD after downloading a few songs. It also demonstrates that P2P promotes albums as radio stations do: file-sharers typically download chart hits. It is recommended that music companies and record labels monitor P2P—instead of discouraging it—to devise new, effective promotional and marketing strategies.

Internet music piracy not only doesn't hurt legitimate CD sales, it may even boost sales of some types of music.

Those were the counterintuitive findings released in March by Harvard Business School [HBS] professor Felix Oberholzer-Gee and his co-author Koleman Strumpf, of the University of North Carolina at Chapel Hill. Their paper, "The Effect of File Sharing on Record Sales," caused a ruckus in the music industry not seen since the British invasion of the Beatles.

Many recording executives were not singing "Yeah, yeah, yeah," however. Convinced that illegal downloading and file

Sean Silverthorne, "Music Downloads—Pirates or Customers?" *Harvard Business School Working Knowledge*, June 21, 2004. Reproduced by permission.

sharing has robbed them of billions of dollars after four consecutive years of falling music sales, they criticized the team's methodology, which consisted of monitoring 1.75 million downloads over 17 weeks in 2002, scouring through server logs from OpenNap (an open source Napster server), and comparing the sales of almost 700 albums as reported by Nielsen SoundScan. Oberholzer and Strumpf concluded that there was almost no relationship between the two.

The number of illegal music downloads continued to increase—but so did music sales.

How could this be? The researchers believe that most downloading is done over peer-to-peer networks by teens and college kids, groups that are "money-poor but time-rich," meaning they wouldn't have bought the songs they downloaded. In that sense, the music industry can't claim those downloads as lost record sales. In fact, illegal downloading may help the industry slightly with another major segment, which Oberholzer and Strumpf call "samplers"—an older crowd who downloads a song or two and then, if they like what they hear, go out and buy the music.

Interestingly, the first half of this year saw the release of numbers seemingly supporting this theory: The number of illegal music downloads continued to increase—but so did music sales.

The Strategic Implications

If in fact the research is correct, the strategic implications for the music industry are profound. Instead of conducting a high-profile campaign against pirates, should the industry instead target "samplers" to encourage them to buy more music? Should the industry consider peer-to-peer services as marketing tools rather than the enemy? Should online pricing be different from in-store pricing? What happens when broadband makes it as easy to illegally download an entire CD as an individual track or two? HBS professor Felix Oberholzer-Gee recently spoke to *Working Knowledge* about these issues.

Sean Silverthorne: The draft of your paper with Koleman Strumpf came out almost three months ago, and caused quite a stir both inside the entertainment industry and out. What are your impressions of the reactions so far?

Felix Oberholzer-Gee: Two recent developments are important. Our study provides the first serious evidence that file sharing cannot explain the decline in music sales in the last couple of years. In addition, in the last two quarters, music sales increased while file sharing has become even more popular. BigChampagne.com, an Internet monitoring firm, estimates that there are now [in 2004] up to 9 million simultaneous file sharers, up from about 4 million in early 2003.

In view of our evidence and these new trends, even the Recording Industry Association of America (RIAA) now states that file sharing is only "one factor, along with economic conditions and competing forms of entertainment that is displacing legitimate sales." The industry is rethinking its position, although change occurs slowly.

Let's talk strategy. What have been the recording companies' strategies to date for combating their loss of property rights via illegal downloading? And how effective has that strategy been? For example, is it a good thing to sue potential customers?

Suing potential customers is not exactly a standard entry in the book of good CRM [customer relationship management]. More importantly, the RIAA's legal strategy is hopeless and smacks of short-sighted panic.

Our research shows that only 45 percent of music files downloaded in the United States come from computers in the U.S. More than 100 countries supply files to the U.S. file-sharing community, and many of these countries do not have strong records of protecting copyrighted materials. The RIAA does not stand a chance to implement an effective legal strategy in all these countries.

Those who dream of legal solutions do not recognize the truly global nature of the peer-to-peer (P2P) phenomenon. Even worse, the RIAA's legal strategy does not even seem to work here in the United States. Despite the lawsuits—the RIAA has sued about 2,000 individuals to date—file sharing is more popular than ever.

Stimulating Sales

Assuming your conclusion is right—that there is no evidence that illegal music downloads erode CD sales—and in fact might help top-selling record sales—what are the implications for the recording industry in terms of strategy?

Our research shows that people do not download entire CDs. They download a few songs, typically the hits that one would also hear on a Top 40 station. This suggests that P2P is much like the radio, a great tool to promote new music. The music industry has of course long recognized that giving away samples of music for free over the airwaves can stimulate sales. The same seems to hold for P2P.

The problem with radio as a promotional tool is that it can be quite expensive for labels to get radio stations to play their music. P2P networks are promising because they make the market for music promotion more competitive. From the perspective of the music industry, the more competition among P2P services, the less costly it will be to promote music.

Apple's iTunes has seemingly validated the concept that people will purchase music online. But it seems the recording companies themselves have done little on their own to experiment with models here, such as tiered pricing (hits cost more) and bundling.

The classic business model was a teaser model: The music labels provided one or two hit songs for free by promoting them on the radio and on MTV. If consumers liked the samples, they purchased a dozen songs at a price of $15. We now have gone from one extreme to the other. While inflexible bundling was the rule, services such as iTunes now completely unbundle CDs and offer all music by the song. The difficulty with this approach is that the economics of producing music are characterized by significant fixed costs. It is not much more expensive to promote an entire album than to promote an individual song. With complete unbundling, the revenue streams generated by a new album are likely to be much lower. How many consumers will pay a dollar for song number thirteen?

Clearly, there is a profit-enhancing role for some type of bundling even with digital distribution. For example, consumers might be willing to pay full price for the core songs on an album if they get the rest at a discount. We need systematic experiments to find out which types of bundling are economically most attractive.

Appropriate in the Digital Age

What's the current state of your research? Where does it go from here?

A key uncertainty relates to our finding that file sharers do not download entire CDs. We do not know why they sample only a few songs. One possibility is that the current patterns of file sharing reflect consumer preferences. Consumers do not know the quality of new music and sampling one or two songs is good enough to assess quality and make a purchasing decision. If this view is correct, the radio model is well and alive, and P2P offers great opportunities to promote new content.

However, it is also possible that the observed behavior is due to technical difficulties. In our data, only one out of three downloads is completed successfully. File sharing is fairly cumbersome for many consumers with poor Internet connections. If this is the reason for highly selective sampling, we can expect consumers to download entire CDs when broadband connections become more common. This is a less rosy scenario for the music industry because downloads of CDs are likely to be closer substitutes for CD purchases.

If poor Internet connections explain file-sharing patterns, general access to broadband would have profound strategic implications, suggesting that music companies ought to pursue a strategy of selling complements to recorded music. We see some examples for this strategy even today: Apple sells songs to promote its iPods. Prince gives away his most recent release to promote his concerts. We need careful continuous monitoring of the effects of P2P to know which strategies are most appropriate in the digital age.

Organizations to Contact

The editors have compiled the following list of organizations concerned with the issues debated in this book. The descriptions are derived from materials provided by the organizations. All have publications or information available for interested readers. The list was compiled on the date of publication of the present volume; the information provided here may change. Be aware that many organizations take several weeks or longer to respond to inquiries, so allow as much time as possible.

American Society of Composers, Authors, and Performers (ASCAP)
One Lincoln Plaza, New York, NY   10023
Web site: www.ascap.com

ASCAP is a membership association of more than 315,000 U.S. composers, songwriters, lyricists, and music publishers of all genres of music. Through agreements with affiliated international societies, ASCAP also represents hundreds of thousands of music creators worldwide. ASCAP is the only U.S. performing rights organization created and controlled by composers, songwriters, and music publishers, with a board of directors elected by and from the membership.

Audio Engineering Society (AES)
60 East 42nd Street, Room 2520, New York, NY
(212) 661-8528 • fax: (212) 682-0477
Web site: www.aes.org

AES is the only professional society devoted exclusively to audio technology. Its membership of engineers, scientists, and other authorities has increased dramatically throughout the world, greatly boosting the society's stature and that of its members. The society publishes a variety of anthologies, conference proceedings, standards, drafts, and other documents.

International Federation of the Phonographic Industry (IFPI)

10 Piccadilly, London   W1J 0DD
   United Kingdom
+44 (0)20 7878 7900 • fax: +44 (0)20 7878 7950
e-mail: info@ifpi.org
Web site: www.ifpi.org

IFPI represents the recording industry worldwide with some 1,400 members in 73 countries and affiliated industry associations in 48 countries. IFPI's international secretariat is based in London and is linked to regional offices in Brussels, Hong Kong, Miami, and Moscow. The federation's mission is to promote the value of recorded music, safeguard the rights of record producers, and expand the commercial uses of recorded music.

Music Publishers' Association (MPA)

243 5th Avenue, Suite 236, New York, NY   10016
e-mail: admin@mpa.org
Web site: www.mpa.org

Founded in 1895, the MPA is the oldest music trade organization in the United States, fostering communication among publishers, dealers, music educators, and all ultimate users of music. This nonprofit association addresses itself to issues pertaining to every area of music publishing with an emphasis on the issues relevant to the publishers of print music for concert and educational purposes.

NAMM, the International Music Products Association

5790 Armada Drive, Carlsbad, CA   92008
(760) 438-8001 • fax: (760) 438-7327
e-mail: info@namm.org
Web site: www.namm.org

Established in 1901 as a small, grassroots organization, NAMM is an international association representing nearly 9,000 retailers and manufacturers of musical instruments and products from 85 countries worldwide. NAMM's mission is to support the global music products industry and increase active participation in music making.

National Association of Record Industry Professionals (NARIP)
P.O. Box 2446, Toluca Lake, CA   91610-2446
(818) 769-7007
Web site: www.narip.com

NARIP promotes education, career advancement, and goodwill among record executives. With an emphasis on educating and informing record executives, NARIP offers professional development opportunities, educational programs and seminars, the opportunity to meet and interact with peers, a job bank, a member resume database for employers, a mentor network, a newsletter, and other services.

National Association of Recording Merchandisers (NARM)
9 Eves Drive, Suite 120, Marlton, NJ   08053
(856) 596-2221 • fax: (856) 596-3268
Web site: www.narm.com

Established in 1958, NARM is a nonprofit trade association that serves the music retailing community in the areas of networking, advocacy, information, education, and promotion. The association's membership includes music and other entertainment retailers, wholesalers, distributors, record labels, multimedia suppliers, and suppliers of related products and services, as well as individual professionals and educators in the music business field.

Recording Industry Association of America (RIAA)
1025 F Street NW, 10th Floor, Washington, DC   20004
(202) 775-0101
Web site: www.riaa.org

RIAA is the trade group that represents the U.S. recording industry. Its mission is to foster a business and legal climate that supports and promotes its members' creative and financial vitality. RIAA members create, manufacture, and/or distribute approximately 90 percent of all legitimate sound recordings produced and sold in the United States.

Women in Music National Network (WIMNN)

1450 Oddstad Drive, Redwood City, CA   94063
(866) 305-7963
Web site: www.womeninmusic.com

Founded in 1993, WIMNN provides a network to support research efforts and opportunities for women in music. Subscriptions, donations, and sponsorships are used to support the organization's goals and objectives, which include its Web site, seminars, mentor programs, newsletter, and a variety of other educational and business activities.

Bibliography

Books

Chris Anderson — *The Long Tail: Why the Future of Business Is Selling Less of More.* New York: Hyperion, 2006.

Moses Avalon — *Confessions of a Record Producer: How to Survive the Scams and Shams of the Music Business,* 3rd ed. San Francisco: Backbeat Books, 2006.

Arthur Bernstein, Naoki Sekine, and Dick Weissman — *The Global Music Industry: Three Perspectives.* New York: Routledge, 2007.

Danny Goldberg — *Bumping into Geniuses: Inside the Rock and Roll Business.* New York: Gotham Books, 2008.

Steve Gordon — *The Future of the Music Business.* San Francisco: Backbeat Books, 2005.

Steven Levy — *The Perfect Thing: How the iPod Shuffles Commerce, Culture, and Coolness.* New York: Simon & Schuster, 2006.

David Kusek and Gerd Leonhard — *The Future of Music.* Boston: Berklee Press, 2005.

David J. Moser — *Moser on Music Copyright.* Swanton, VT: Artistpro, 2005.

Donald S. Passman — *All You Need to Know About the Music Business*, 6th ed. New York: Free Press, 2006.

Richard Schulenberg — *Legal Aspects of the Music Industry.* New York: Billboard Books, 2005.

Periodicals

Ed Christman — "Paper or Plastic: Jewelboxes Lose Their Luster," *Billboard*, March 29, 2008.

J. Freedom du Lac — "His Bombastic Attacks Keep the Music Industry on Its Toes," *Boston Globe*, April 1, 2008.

Jon Healey — "File Sharing: To Fight or Accommodate?" *Los Angeles Times*, April 1, 2008.

Jeff Leeds — "Does This Latte Have a Funny Mainstream Taste to You?" *New York Times*, March 17, 2008.

Karen Lowry Miller — "A Different Tune: How EMI and Other Music-Industry Giants Are Fighting Back Against Digital Rivals, Pirates, and Freeloaders," *Newsweek*, October 17, 2005.

Music Trades — "Measuring the Global Market," *Music Trades*, December 2007.

Ken C. Pohlmann — "Dark Side of the Tune: Sound Quality Is on the Run," *Sound & Vision*, July–August 2006.

David Polochanin   "Static All the Way," *Christian Science Monitor*, December 11, 2007.

Andrew Potter   "No One Likes to Pay for Music—or Much Else," *Maclean's*, February 25, 2008.

Ann Powers   "Music Industry Rules Are Shifting Under Feet of Artists, Fans, and Critics," *Los Angeles Times*, March 26, 2008.

Jeff Price   "The Democratization of the Music Industry," *Huffington Post*, March 11, 2008.

Adam Smith   "The Music Industry: Lost in the Shuffle," *Time*, March 19, 2008.

Joanne Taffe   "TME: DRM and Copyright: Rights Issues," *Total Telecom Magazine*, April 1, 2008.

John C. Tanner   "Cracking the Mobile Music Puzzle," *Wireless Asia*, June 2006.

Lance Ulanoff   "DRM-free Music Spells Trouble," *PC Magazine*, March 2008.

Index

A

A & M Records v. Napster, Inc., 64
Adams, Sean, 44
Advertising and promotion
    CDs as, 11
    classic business model and, 73
    digital downloads as, 24, 26, 27, 29
    piracy as, 69–74
    radio and, 18, 26, 28, 29, 72
Advertising-supported free music downloads, 21
Aimster, 63, 66
Aimster Copyright Litigation, 63
Albom, Mitch, 54
All Access Group (AAC), 27, 41
Amazon.com, 19, 20, 21, 52, 53–54, 57
American Idol (TV program), 12
American Society of Composers, Authors, and Performers (ASCAP), 75
Amory, Patrick, 56
Anderson, Hil, 31–34
Apple Inc.
    competition with Amazon, 21
    digital downloads and, 20, 72–73
    iPod sales, 11
    unlimited music plan, 8
    See also iTunes
Arcade Fire (music group), 29
ASCAP (American Society of Composers, Authors, and Performers), 75
Ashworth, Chris, 57
Audio Engineering Society (AES), 75

Auditory fatigue, 41, 42, 43
Auto industry, 53

B

Babcock, Joshua, 58
Bankruptcies, 14, 33
Barnes & Noble, 54
Beah, Ishmael, 54
Bearshare, 66
Beatles, 49
Berg, Alban, 54
Berklee College of Music, 24, 47
Bernstein & Company, 48
Bernstein, Sanford C., 34
Best Buy Co., 13, 15, 32
BigChampagne LLC, 13, 71
Black, Clint, 48
Bocelli, Andrea, 52
Borders bookstores, 46, 54
Borst, Drew, 48
Bracy, Michael, 20–21, 26–27, 29
Bridge Ratings, 25
British Phonographic Industry, 23
Brooks, Carey, 48
Brumelle, Colin, 23
Byrne, David, 21

C

Carey, Mariah, 53
Cassette tapes, 16, 17, 23, 67
CDs
    as advertisement, 11
    compression and, 39–41, 56–57
    copying of, 67–68
    decline in sales of, 7, 12, 23, 24

digital sales affecting CD sales, 12

dynamic range and, 35–37, 56–57

marketing method shifts and, 51–54

mastering, 39–41

as obsolete, 41–50, 46–50

price affecting sales of, 33–34, 46

unbundling of, 73

vinyl records as competition for, 55–58

See also iTunes; Music sales

Chain stores

Best Buy Co., 13, 15, 32

f.y.e. stores, 14, 32

Hastings Entertainment, 32

Virgin Megastores, 13

Wherehouse Records, 31–33

See also Tower Records

Charles, Ray, 54

Christian Science Monitor (newspaper), 46

CNET, 55

Coconuts (record store), 14

Cohen, Leonard, 46

Compact Disk. *See* CDs

Compression

CDs and, 39–41, 56–57

explanation of, 36–37

overcompression, 36–37, 39–42, 44

vinyl records and, 37–39

ComScore, 21

Comstock, Jerry, 31, 33

Concert tours, 11, 27–28

Connelly, Ian, 55–56

Consumer Electronics Association, 58

Copyright Act, 64–65

Copyright infringement lawsuits, 63–66

Cryan, Dan, 26

D

Data-compression techniques, 41

Daughtry, Chris, 12

de Barros, Paul, 52

Diddy, 18

Digital downloads

as advertising and promotion tool, 24, 26, 27, 29

advertising-supported free music downloads, 21

Amazon.com and, 20

Apple Inc. and, 20

Echo and, 31–33

escalation of, 23, 24

permitable downloads, 66–67

as radio replacement, 20

"samplers," 70

See also Internet; Piracy

Digital music, future of, 20–30

Direct Stream Digital, 43

Distribution models, 20

Downloads. *See* Digital downloads

Dreamgirls (movie soundtrack), 12

Dupri, Jermaine, 11

DVD-Audio, 43

Dynamic range, 35–37, 56–57

E

Echo (record store group), 31–33

Edison, Thomas, 23

Effect of File Sharing on Record Sales (Oberholzer-Gee and Strumpf), 69–70

eMarketer, 22, 27

EMI, 41

F

Faber, Peter, 22, 29

Facebook (social network), 26, 28

FBI warnings, 59–60

Financial Times (newspaper), 8

FLAC (Free Lossless Audio Code), 41, 43–44

Forrester, 24

Fortune (magazine), 21

Free Lossless Audio Code (FLAC), 41, 43–44

Free Republic, L.A. Times v., 66

Future of Music Coalition, 20

Future of Music (Kusek), 24

f.y.e. stores, 14, 32

G

Gallery of Sound, 14

Geffen Records, 8

Gnutella, 66

Google of music business, 29–30

Gorter, Don, 47

Graves, Michael, 49, 50

Green Day (music group), 18, 35

Greenfield, Richard, 14

Griffin, Jim, 8

Groban, Josh, 52, 54

Grokster, 66

Guru (musician), 19

H

Hart, Dan, 32

Harvard Business School, 69

Hastings Entertainment, 32

High-fidelity format, 43

HMV, 53

Hoffman, Steve, 42–43

Honey Cone, 38

"Hot" mastering, 38–40

I

Il Divo (music group), 52

Illegal music downloads. *See* Piracy

Intellectual Reserve, Inc. v. Utah Lighthouse Ministry, Inc., 66

International Federation of the Phonographic Industry (IFPI), 76

Internet

    discovery of new music and, 24, 26

    Internet service providers (ISPs), 8

    music business model and, 26–28, 31–33

    music revenues and, 28

    music supply and, 11

    surcharges for payment of music downloads, 8, 26

    See also Digital downloads

IODA (independent music distributor alliance), 56

iPods, 11, 41, 45, 52

iTunes

    CD sales and, 53

    increase in sales, 10, 72–73

    as innovative, 12

    instant purchases, 18

    normalization option, 45

    percentage of music sales, 7

    See also Apple Inc; CDs; Music sales

J

Jones, Norah, 14

K

Katz, Bob, 39

Kazaa, 66

Kelis (musician), 11

Keys, Alicia, 18

Kinder, Seth, 46, 50

Kusek, David, 24, 26, 27

L

L.A. Times v. Free Republic, 66
Lamy, Jonathan, 57
LaPlante, Alice, 20–30
Lawsuits, 8, 63–66, 71
Leeds, Jeff, 51–52
Lefsetz, Bob, 29
Lefsetz Letter, 29
LimeWire, 66
Listen.com, 49
Loggins & Messina, 17
Logitech, 44
Loudness war
    dynamic range and, 35, 56–57
    high-fidelity formats and, 43
    overcompression of dynamic
      range and, 36–37
    Replay Gain and, 45
Lycos Rhapsody, 49

M

MacInnis, Don, 57
Madonna (musician), 18
Mastering
    CDs, 39–41
    "hot" mastering, 38–40
    vinyl records, 37–39, 42
Matador (record label), 56
Matchbox Twenty, 7
Mayer, John, 18
McCartney, Paul, 52
McNamara, Patrick, 57
McQuivey, James, 24
Merchandise, 7, 11, 27
Microsoft, 8
Morpheus (online service), 48, 66
Morton, Samantha, 28
Morveau, Chris, 16–19
Motion Picture Association of
    America (MPAA), 8
Motown Records, 38

MP3 format
    blogs for, 16
    CD decline and, 41
    compression and, 44
    as detrimental to music in-
      dustry, 23
    Napster and, 32–33
    piracy and, 16, 59, 61
MP3.com, UMG Recordings, Inc. v.,
    64
MTV, 20, 29
Murphy, Samantha, 22
Music business model, 26–28,
    31–33
Music consumption growth, 24–26
Music Publishers' Association
    (MPA), 76
Music sales
    decline in, 7, 10–15, 51
    direct sales by artists, 9, 18,
      20, 21, 48
    format changes and, 17, 55–58
    Napster and, 29
    piracy and, 58–74
    poor content and, 16–19
    price effecting sales, 33–34, 46
    as product, 22–24
    as service, 22–24
    See also CDs; iTunes; Sales
      statistics
Musicland Holding Corp., 14
MySpace, 11, 26, 28

N

Nadones, Joe Jr., 14
NAMM, International Music
    Products Association, 76–77
Napster, 13, 29, 32, 47, 64, 70
Napster, Inc., A & M Records v., 64
Nathanson, Michael, 33–34
National Association of Record
    Industry Professionals (NARIP),
    77

National Association of Recording Merchandisers (NARM), 77
NET Act, 62–63
New York Times, 34, 52
Newspapers, 11–12
Nielsen SoundScan, 12, 24, 58, 70
No Electronic Theft Law (NET Act), 62–63
Numark, 58
Nyquist's theorem, 57

O

Oberholzer-Gee, Felix, 69–71
Ohio v. Perry, 65
Overcompression of dynamic range, 36–37, 39–42, 44

P

Pali Research, 13, 14
PCM (pulse code modulation), 39, 43
Peer-to-peer (P2P) file sharing, 7, 59, 61–63, 69–74
Penalties for piracy, 8, 49–50, 59–60, 62–63
Perry, Ohio v., 65
Philips, 39, 43
Pink Floyd, 35, 49
Piracy
    as advertising, 69–74
    consciousness raising and, 50
    escalation of, 7, 13
    examples of, 61–62
    file-sharing networks and, 13
    lawsuits and, 8, 63–66, 71
    lost sales and, 19
    Napster and, 13, 29, 32–33, 47
    penalties for, 8, 49–50, 59–60, 62–63
    permissible downloads, 66–67
    piracy tax, 8
    as shoplifting, 50

"spoofing" and, 49–50
    as threat to music industry, 59–68
    as worldwide, 47–48
Pitchfork (online music site), 29
Playboy Enterprises v. Russ Hardenburgh, Inc., 64
Playboy Enterprises v. Webbworld Inc. 65
Playing for Profit: How Digital Entertainment Is Making Big Business Out of Child's Play (LaPlante), 20
Profit margins, 24
Pulse code modulation (PCM), 39, 43

Q

Quality. *See* Sound quality

R

Rabban, Jeff, 11
Radio
    digital downloads as replacement for, 20
    early negative perceptions of, 23
    as music-promotion tool, 18, 26, 28, 29, 72
Radiohead (music group), 9, 18, 20, 21
Rasputin (record store), 53
RCRD LBL (online record label), 8–9
Record Technology (record pressing plant), 57
Recording Industry Association of America (RIAA)
    CD sales statistics and, 51
    contact information for, 77–78
    lawsuits regarding piracy, 7–8

music industry economic conditions, 59–68, 71–72
vinyl resurgence and, 57
Red Hot Chili Peppers, 42
Replay Gain, 45
Rhapsody (online music site), 20
RIAA. *See* Recording Industry Association of America (RIAA)
Richards, Kelli, 27–29
Ringtones, 12
Ritholtz, Barry, 53
RMS (root mean square), 40
Rolling Stone (magazine), 20, 29
Rolling Stones (music group), 18, 27
Roman, Chris, 58
Root mean square (RMS), 40
Royalties, 26
Russ Hardenburgh, Inc., Playboy Enterprises v., 64

S

Sabella, Sega Enterprises v., 65
Sales statistics
   2006 and 2007 compared, 16–17
   CD sales, 51
   digital sales effecting CD sales, 12
   and illegal music downloads, 7
   profit margins and, 24
   See also CDs; Music sales
Sam Goody (record store), 14
"Samplers," 70
Screen Digest (media company), 26, 27
Seattle Times, 52
Sega Enterprises v. Sabella, 65
Silver Platters (CD stores), 52, 53
Silverthorne, Sean, 69
Single-concept albums, 46, 49
Slim Devices, 44

Smith, Ethan, 10–15
Social networking, 26
Society of Rockets (music group), 58
Sony BMG, 41
Sony Entertainment, 39, 43, 47
Sound Check (sound modification), 45
Sound quality
   auditory fatigue, 41, 42, 43
   CDs, 39–41
   compression and, 36–37
   definitive peak loudness, 39
   overcompression and, 36–37, 39–42, 44
   overview of decline in, 35–36
   subscription-based music services, 49
   vinyl records and, 37–39, 56–57
Sousa, John Philip, 23
"Spoofing," 49–50
Squeezebox (digital music product), 44
Sreedhar, Suhas, 35–45
Starbucks, 52, 54
Steven Institute of Technology, 35
Stewart, Rod, 54
Strumpf, Koleman, 69, 71
Subscription-based music services
   growth in, 20, 47–48
   as music producers, 26
   reasons for not subscribing, 48–49
   record companies and, 47
   sound quality and, 49
Subscription services, 12
Super Audio Compact Disc (SACD), 43

T

T-shirts, 11
Thomas, Jamie, 8
Timberlake, Justin, 18

Tours, 11, 27–28

Tower Records
    advertising expenditures, 53
    bankruptcy filing, 14
    decline of, 10, 11, 13, 19, 51, 52
    Echo and, 32
    See also Chain stores

Trans World Entertainment Corp., 14

Transporter, 44

Turntables, 54, 57

U

U2, 18

UMG Recordings, Inc. v. MP3.com, Inc., 64

United Press International, 31

United Record Pressing, 57

Universal Music Group, 41, 47

Universal serial bus (USB) drives, 7

University of North Carolina, 69

University of Pennsylvania, 22

Unlimited music plan, 8

USB turntables, 57

Utah Lighthouse Ministry, Inc., Intellectual Reserve, Inc. v., 66

V

Verna, Paul, 22, 25, 27, 30

Vinyl records, 37–39, 42, 55–58

Virgin Megastores, 13, 32

W

Wal-Mart stores, 7, 13, 15

Wall Street Journal, 10, 51

Warner Music Group Corp., 8, 13, 41

Webbworld Inc., Playboy Enterprises v., 65

Wharton School of Business, 22

Wherehouse Music, 31, 33

White Stripes, 7

Winamp, 45

WinMX, 66

Wired (magazine), 21

Women in Music National Network (WIMNN), 78

Wood, Daniel B., 46–50

Working Knowledge (magazine), 71

Wright, Simon, 13

Y

Yamin, Elliott, 11

Yorke, Thom, 21

YouTube, 28

Z

Zune, 8